DECKONOMICS

Deckonomics: Develop presentations that spread ideas, drive decisions and close deals.

Published by Gatekeeper Press
7853 Gunn Hwy., Suite 209
Tampa, FL 33626
www.GatekeeperPress.com

Library of Congress Control Number: 2021943771

ISBN (paperback): 9781662915109
eISBN: 9781662915116

DECKONOMICS

Develop presentations that spread ideas,
drive decisions and close deals.

GINGER ZUMAETA

gatekeeper press™
Tampa, Florida

For Stacie, for all the reasons . . .
and the reasons beyond reason.

Introduction

You can achieve nearly impossible things with slide presentations if you learn how to do them properly. How do I know? Because the evidence is all around us. You've probably heard of *An Inconvenient Truth*, the PowerPoint that became a documentary that went on to receive an Academy Award and nabbed Al Gore the Nobel Peace Prize. That's impact on a global scale. But, while the likelihood of someone making a movie out of your slide deck is probably infinitesimally small, there are legions of people who've launched or saved projects and programs worth millions and sometimes billions of dollars based on a well-structured and well-designed slide deck. I've had the privilege of working with some of them, and I assure you that the gap between their decks and yours is closable. At the

risk of sounding evangelical, I'm here to tell you that you can change lives and even save lives with a PowerPoint deck —easily, if you know how. That's what I'm going to share with you.

Here's my guess. The reason you picked up this book is that **you've realized your slide decks need to get better.** It could be that you're not getting the outcomes you want when you pitch your ideas. Maybe you feel like others still aren't "getting it" after you finish your presentation. Or, maybe you've seen someone else's deck that has inspired you to up your game. No worries, you've come to the right place. This book is a step-by-step guide for building powerfully persuasive presentations.

PowerPoints (slides, presentations, decks) are the language of business. It's through these documents that business gets done today. But sadly, few people are trained to put decks together in the right way, especially for workaday presentations. There's a pattern to creating decks that influence, but it's seldom taught. In this book, you're going to learn about the Hero's Journey and why your pitch deck is the magic wand that gets the person you're pitching to cross the threshold. You'll learn that presentations are nothing more than business stories, and the person with the best story wins. It's your ability to tell a compelling story—one that paints a picture of a better future—that determines whether your pitch will motivate action.

Approximately **three hundred and seventy million dollars are wasted every day on PowerPoint.**[1] And that's just PowerPoint. It doesn't include Keynote, or Google Slides, or Prezi, or whatever other slideware is in fashion. It's a conservative estimate. People in organizations spend way too much time either preparing decks or suffering through them, often with no end result. What a waste. Developing a PowerPoint is pointless (pun intended) if nothing happens afterward.

---

[1] This is an estimate. Microsoft did an extensive study in 2001, estimating the number at $250 million per day, and I've updated that number to today's value.

Here's who will benefit from this book:

► **Sales and marketing professionals** who aren't getting the outcomes they need from pitches

► **Corporate executives** who need to accelerate pushing the right work forward

► **Medical or scientific professionals** who have a hard time explaining the complexities of what they work on to folks who are less conversant in their particular field of expertise

► **Founders or start-up folks** who need to develop a pitch deck to share with potential investors or early adopters

► **Students** who want to ace their class projects

► **Consultants** who trade on putting their thoughts to paper to summarize their thinking and recommendations.

What this book will do is give you an understanding of the basic ingredients of persuasion and a framework to build your decks as stories so they are as effective as possible.

This book is organized to help you master the 5 Laws of Powerful Presentations:

1.   STORY STRUCTURE
2.   SUCCINCT
3.   SCANNABLE
4.   STICKY
5.   SHAREABLE

The 5 Laws Of Powerful Presentations

01	**Structured as Stories**	Presentations structured as stories are inherently persuasive.
02	**Succinct**	Decks that have an economy to them are more clearly understood. (Yep, that's where the title Deckonomics came from.)
03	**Scannable**	Documents that are easy to consume guarantee that your audience will get the entire gist of what you're trying to communicate.
04	**Sticky**	The key to making your message memorable is creating the conditions for an emotional response and adding memorable visuals.
05	**Sharable**	Your message is more likely to spread if it's packaged correctly, with all the right metadata.

Part 1 of this book focuses on the narrative, where you'll master the first two laws. The person with the best story wins. When you learn how to tell a story through a slide deck, you will have harnessed an almost magical power to transform other people's thinking and behavior. And you'll be surprised how your own thinking and behavior changes as well. Part 2 focuses on packaging your story into a deck that people will love and want to share.

I spent the first half of my career in television. As vice president of advertising and promotion at NBC & Telemundo, it was my job to tantalize viewers into watching more of their favorite shows and to checking out new ones. It was there that I learned the power of storytelling and of sparking people's emotions to influence behaviors. When I left television, I used these same skills in my consulting practice to help companies tell brand stories, and now, I train business leaders to do this themselves. One of the most gratifying things I've experienced training professionals to create better presentations is that it simultaneously helps them become expert communicators. Start using the principles in this book and others will start seeing you as a domain expert and clear-thinking strategist. That gives you a lot of power!

If you're ready to learn how to build a deck that gets to the point with clarity and concision and that is persuasive so you can get people to understand, remember, and want to spread your ideas—read on. You're about to learn something that will completely change the game.

How to Use This Book

▶ **As an *overall presentation* manual:** Folks who spend a good amount of time building presentations—whether they're for persuasion or knowledge transfer—should read this book cover to cover.

▶ **As a *strategic storytelling* manual:** Those who need to improve their business storytelling skills will particularly benefit from part 1.

▶ **As a presentation *production* manual:** Those who need to improve the look and feel of their presentations will particularly benefit from part 2.

▶ **As a subtle hint:** If you manage people who create presentations and need your team to up-level their skills, gift this book to them!

HELPFUL TERMS

▶ *PowerPoint, slideware,* and *software* are terms used interchangeably throughout the book to represent the tool used to create the presentation.

▶ *PowerPoint, presentation, deck, pitch,* and *slide* are used interchangeably when I'm talking about the document (the artifact) as opposed to the tool.

▶ I'll also use *graphics, visuals,* and *images* interchangeably.

▶ Finally, I'll use the word copy when I refer to the text of the document. (Yes, you'll begin to think of yourself as a copywriter and author.)

DISCLAIMERS

Before you get started, know this:

1. **I will not be telling you how to use PowerPoint or suggesting any templates.** That's a fool's errand. That would be like saying the bottle is more important than the rare wine it contains. It would emphasize the container over its contents.

2. **I also won't teach you how to be a better public speaker or to develop TED-style presentations that rely heavily on the charm and authority of the speaker.** Instead, you'll learn to build business presentations that can stand on their own, often without the benefit of a voice-over.

3. **I will teach you to think and communicate better** in the form where business really happens—slides!

Chapter 1
The Power of Stories

The only way for your content to be **understood, remembered, retold and acted upon** is to structure it as a story.

I never could have guessed I'd have a career in TV that included meeting Oprah, winning three Emmy Awards, and taking three of the nation's top television stations in the country to a number one position in their markets. I started out in TV research in the nineties in San Antonio, Texas. At that time, the role was designed solely to support the sales function. In other words, my job was to predict the number of people who would be watching a TV program on any given day and time . . . in order to justify the price we would ask for those "eyeballs." But the more I studied the numbers, the more I learned to use them to tell stories not only to predict our ratings, but to grow them.

When I started building presentations to recommend changes, and when my recommendations started paying off, my general manager (GM) made the unconventional move of taking me out of the research director seat and placing me in the marketing director seat. The rest is history. Those research presentations are what pivoted me into a successful marketing career—first in television, and ultimately into running my own brand strategy firm.

What's Your Story?

What's the most pivotal decision you ever made in your professional life—the one that got you to right now? What about your most important accomplishment last year? How about the biggest decision you made last week? There's a story behind the answer to every one of those questions.

Stories are how we process what we learn and how we retrieve the information later. Think about the most important day of your life.

The saddest moment. The happiest moment. If you were telling these stories out loud, they would be told as stories with complete sentences. Here's what they *wouldn't* be—bullet points.

And so, **if you want to build an effective presentation—a *persuasive* presentation—you have to be able to tell a story that your audience can follow easily**. To do that, you need to understand the mechanics at work. The good news is that stories have very predictable structures and when you use a story-based narrative structure to build out your slide deck, you'll be able to hold your audience's attention. They'll be able to remember what you said, and they'll follow your logic. But most importantly, they'll feel comfortable taking action. It was the reason my GM in San Antonio was motivated to promote me into the marketing role.

There Are Really Only Two Types of Presentations: Informative and Persuasive

When you think about why you're creating your presentation, it's probably for one of just a handful of reasons that fall into two major categories. The first category is **conveying information**. This would include presentations that provide information, teach a skill, or report progress. For example, perhaps you are updating the leadership team on a project. Why is it important to update them in the first place? Think about it for a minute. Somebody wants to know how things are progressing toward a goal. *Is the project on track? Will the way you're doing it work? Why is it delayed? Why is it costing more than you expected?* All of those are stories. By the end of your presentation, you want your audience to hold a particular point of view on the topic. **Informational presentations still tell a story either implicitly or explicitly.**

The second category of presentations aims toward **influencing an action or decision**. These are the presentations that seek to sell an idea, product, or service. Or they seek a decision. **They include a request to do something**. In these cases you need buy-in. You need a key person to make a decision based on the information and logic you are supplying.

In today's world, **slide decks are the language of business**. But most of the time, they SUCK! Way back in 2001, Seth Godin wrote an eBook called *Really Bad PowerPoint (and How to Avoid It)*. In that book he detailed all the things that go wrong in slide presentations. I'm sure he didn't imagine back then that the problem would only have continued to grow. Presentation software and preloaded templates have exacerbated the problem.

"Communication is
the transfer of
emotion... about
getting others to
adopt your point of
view. If all you want to
do is create a file of
facts and figures, then
cancel the meeting
and send in a report."

— Seth Godin

To create truly impactful
slide decks, you need
to get to the point with
clarity and logic,
but also emotion, and
the best way to do that
is through stories.

Stories And The Hero's Journey

Stories work because of two things: 1) the way we structure them, and 2) the way your brain works. Stories have instructed, guided, and persuaded people since before the written word existed. In fact, it's the ability to use language to tell stories that separates us from all other species.

When you think of the oldest stories—the Epic of Gilgamesh, Odysseus returning from the Trojan War, David and Goliath, Jesus's Sermon on the Mount, or the story of Buddha under the bodhi tree—these stories were told, remembered, and passed down because they made people feel something. Think of Abraham Lincoln's Emancipation Proclamation and Martin Luther King Jr's dream speech. They designed those speeches to touch the imagination in order to shift opinions. The reason we remember these speeches is that they all contain elements that ignited—and still ignite—our imaginations. **They all follow a blueprint.**

And so, when you think of authoring a slide presentation, you need to be thoughtful about using the structures that turn them from mere collections of facts and hypotheses into a story.

To understand the mechanics of storytelling, it helps to be familiar with the *universal* story, the monomyth, the Hero's Journey as articulated by Joseph Campbell. If you're not familiar with Campbell's work directly, you're definitely familiar with the work that he has influenced, the most notable of which is probably *Star Wars*. George Lucas reproduced the steps of the Hero's Journey so closely that he even went as far as calling Campbell "my Yoda."[2] And Lucas isn't the only one. *The Matrix, The Lord of the Rings, The Hunger Games,* the Harry Potter stories—just about every wildly successful epic story ever told has followed the blueprint of the Hero's Journey. Why? Because using the steps of the journey speaks to us at levels that are hard to put into words. We love those stories because we relate to the unlikely heroes Luke Skywalker, Neo, Frodo, Katniss Everdeen, etc. They were normal everyday people until they weren't. Just like us.

So what exactly is the Hero's Journey? Well, without going into Campbell's findings too deeply (though you certainly could!),[3] it's the idea that if you look at the structure of all stories that have endured from the beginning of time, you see a common set of elements that are always arranged in a particular pattern. **The Hero's Journey is a sort of master blueprint.** *Star Wars (Episode IV)* is a great reflection of the Hero's Journey at work.

[2] Bancks, Tristan. "Beyond the hero's journey: 'Joseph [Campbell] is my Yoda.'—George Lucas (1)." Australian Screen Education, no. 33, 2003, p. 32+. Gale Academic OneFile, link.gale.com/apps/doc/A112130487/AON-E?u=anon~828686ed&sid=googleScholar&xid=26a54065. Accessed 8 Aug. 2021.
[3] Do yourself a favor and check out either Campbell's *The Man With A Thousand Faces,* or *The Hero's Journey,* or even the PBS series *The Power of Myth,* where Bill Moyers interviewed Campbell.

1. Luke Skywalker lives on a farm.
2. He finds a secret message in R2D2.
3. Luke initially refuses Obi Wan.
4. Luke's aunt and uncle are killed. He returns to Obi Wan.
5. Luke commits to learning the way of the Force.
6. Luke teams up with Han Solo, and fights off the enemy.
7. They are captured by the Death Star.
8. They find Leia, only to get stuck in a giant trash compactor.
9. They survive, and begin their escape with Princess Leia.
10. They head to the rebel base, with the enemy in pursuit.
11. Luke joins the rebel alliance, and uses the Force to destroy the Death Star.
12. Luke emerges as a hero, and acknowledges the power of the Force.

Ordinary World
Call To Adventure
Refusing the Call
Meet The Mentor
Cross The Thresold
Trials, Allies & Enemies
The Dragon's Den
The Ordeal
Seize The Treasure
The Road Home
Resurrection
The Boon

Do you see the pattern there? Once you see it, you can't unsee it. A person is going through their everyday life. Then something happens that sends them out to accomplish a task. When they set off to accomplish the task, they experience setbacks and wins along the way. If they accomplish the task, not only do they have a new sense of achievement, but they're also able to share their accomplishment and how they did it. And they have a story to tell.

Stories in the Context of Presentations

OK, you get it. Stories are important. But the cool thing is that it has everything to do with how your brain works. In fact, there are many new discoveries in neurobiology that prove that using stories boosts oxytocin, sometimes called the "cuddle" hormone based on the role it plays in producing feelings of trust and bonding.[4] Oxytocin helps people remember key points of your presentation, recall them, and act on those points.

In short, *stories make people care* and put them in a state to be more cooperative. There are extensive empirical studies that reveal that **leaders who tell stories are more effective and go further in their careers.**[5] So think about that for a minute. If prominent leaders use stories as part of their leadership toolbox, why wouldn't you use stories when presenting and interacting with them?

If you need a decision, funding, or approval to move forward with a new initiative, there is an abundance of evidence supporting using story structure, and **building up your storytelling chops is the first and most important skill you can master to build better presentations.** After all, in order for your intended audience to make a decision, they have to tell themselves a story about why they made that decision. Your job is to get them to the point of the decision.

[4] Why Your Brain Loves Good Storytelling, HBR.org 2014.
[5] Ready, Douglas A. *How Storytelling Builds Next-Generation Leaders.* MITSloan Management Review. July 15, 2002

Every time you pitch something, you're casting your audience as heroes who must solve a problem in order to fulfill their quest. You're also casting yourself as the guide who motivates them to take action. In other words, you're the Obi-Wan to their Luke. So before you even start putting together your pitch, you've got to get a few things right.

1. **You must accurately *identify the Hero***—the key person in your *audience*. You, or your product or service, are NOT the Hero. When pitches fail, it's almost always because the presenter gets this first step wrong.

2. **You must know *what the Hero really desires*.**

3. **You must know *what stands in the Hero's way* of getting what they desire.**

4. **You must realize that *YOU are the mentor* who will guide the way.**

5. And finally, for the Hero to prevail, **you must persuade them to first *cross the threshold*.** In other words, the Hero must answer your call to action.

I didn't realize it at the time, but when I started creating PowerPoint presentations for my GM, what I was really doing was showing him (my Hero) some things that needed to change (things standing in the way) that would result in us getting higher ratings (what the Hero really desired). That's what made him take the bold action to move me out of research and into marketing—a move that was so uncommon, he had to get the blessing from the TV station owners. I had armed my GM with the story he needed to cross the threshold and complete his quest.

Stories create emotions and activate the brain at a subconscious level that makes us feel things. And when we feel things, we make decisions such as yes or no, move forward or retreat, spread an idea or bury it. **When you structure your deck as a story, you create the space for your audience to feel something, to have a new clarity about the path forward, and to make a decision.** And that's what you're after.

But don't get me wrong. It's not always easy. If you mess up who your Hero is or what they want, you don't have a chance at being successful.

Key Takeaways & Homework

▶ Stories are how we process the world. They create feeling, memory, and understanding.

▶ Always remember that your audience is your Hero, and you are the mentor.

▶ The reason you're creating a presentation is to move a story forward—to get your key stakeholders to cross the threshold.

▶ Stories create the conditions to influence minds—not only about the work you're presenting but also about you as a credible authority on the content you present.

▶ Why are you developing your presentation?

▶ Who will you be presenting it to?

▶ Why should the audience care about what you have to say?

Chapter 2
Getting into the Right Frame of Mind

To design a presentation that will persuade, enter the mind of the Hero and **answer the question at the heart of the person's quest.**

Presenting is marketing, and marketing is presenting. Despite having worked in marketing for most of my career, this truth didn't really click until I launched my own strategic marketing company. When I started to sell marketing strategy, I had to become very good at presenting to companies why they should pay me good money to do it. In other words, I had to market (via presentations) the marketing. And once my prospects became clients, I had to continue to market the strategies, tactics, processes, and solutions I was delivering. If done right, presentations market your ideas, information, and recommendations.

You are the Mentor with the Map

In the last chapter we covered why stories are so effective for influence, and one thing you learned was the importance of thinking about your primary audience as the Hero. What is a Hero exactly? A Hero is always on a quest for something, but has to overcome obstacles to get it. In order to overcome the obstacles, a guide or mentor is needed, and that's where you come into the story. **You are the mentor who will give counsel to the Hero on how they should proceed on the quest.** You are there to show the Hero the path. And to do that, you'll have to supply a map or directions, or sometimes both.

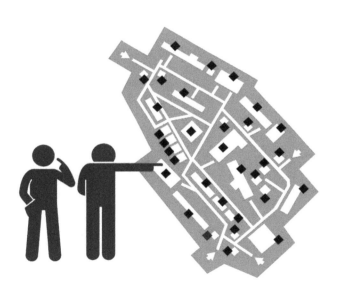

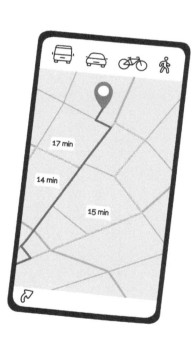

Now, think about a map for a minute. There are two kinds of maps that you'll commonly encounter. One map you'll often see is the "you are here" type of map that orients you to where you are, kind of like those giant maps you see in malls. In presentations, these are your status updates or project reports. They're informational and thus don't have an overt request, but they are important nevertheless because they help key stakeholders orient themselves to how progress is coming along on a project.

Another type of map is the one you see on your car's GPS or on apps like Waze. Those tell you **how to get somewhere**. In presentations, these are the ones designed to *influence*. There are many ways to get from A to B. When driving, you may prefer surface streets, or the shortest distance, or the fastest route. Each of those "ways" would take you on a different route,

depending on your preferences. In other words, once you set your preferences (the rules), your GPS is kind of driving you. You think you're in charge. Your hands are on the wheel. Your foot is on the gas pedal. But apps like Waze are whispering in your ear like Yoda, "Go this way."

So let's think about what type of map you need to create for your Hero. Whether you're putting together an informational or persuasive deck, to design the best map, **you need to answer the following two questions**.

1. Who is the primary Hero?
2. What is the central question your Hero needs to answer?

Let's break down how to answer the first question.

Who Is the Primary Hero?

To design a presentation that delivers your Hero to their desired destination, you need to determine who the Hero of your story really is. This is where a lot of folks get stuck, and that's because the answer isn't always obvious. In business, especially in B2B businesses, the answer can be nuanced because your *presentation's* Hero could work on behalf of a customer or client Hero. Here's one way to simplify: **Who is the person whom you must persuade to cross the threshold?** Who has the power to make a decision that will knock over the first domino that knocks over all the subsequent dominos?

While your presentation may in fact check the boxes for an entire cast of characters, you'll produce a better presentation if you identify a single Hero for the map you're creating. **The reason it's so important to identify a single person is because you will need to unpack what that individual's journey is really about**. There will be *questions* at the heart of their *quest* that you must answer. The presentation's job will be to answer those questions.

But what about the others in the room? In most situations in business, you will have an audience of more than one, as opposed to a single reader or listener. And each of those people will have their own agenda that accords with their role. That means they have their own journey. Still, whose quest are you there to help guide? If you could only have one reader, or make your presentation to only one person—the one that has the power and influence to push this particular story forward—who would that person be? That's your Hero. That's whose mind you need to enter now.

Around our office, we talk about this in terms of the "Hero's Mind." Most of the time, the purpose of your presentation is to get some sort of decision. It could be an explicit or "hard" decision, such as approval to move forward with a project, approval for funds, a headcount, or what have you. Or it could be an implicit or "soft" decision. For example, it could be support or endorsement of a new initiative or buy-in on a plan to change the status quo. Either way, you're looking for a nod from **the person whose nod will influence others' nods. That's who we're talking about when we talk about the Hero's Mind**.

The reason it's so important to enter the Hero's Mind is because **the more you internalize that your presentation is there to serve *their needs,* and to help them deliver *their outcome,* and to push them further along on *their quest,* the better your presentation is going to go**. The other thing you need to remember in terms of the Hero's mind is that your Hero is busy and you are but a single part of that person's larger story. So the Hero doesn't need to know every minor fact that you've gathered or every little step you've taken to get to your conclusion. **What the Hero is looking for from you is the wisdom and the insight of the mentor.**

Think about Yoda. Yoda did not yawn on and on to Luke with histrionics about his résumé and all the battles he fought as a Jedi warrior. His words were few and packed a punch. And that's what you must do. **The reason you're there is to give the Hero a shortcut to the destination.** It's not to recount all the potential routes to the destination, but to supply the one best route.

In most cases, your Hero will be an executive in charge of decision-making, and most **executives today are short on time and under immense pressure and responsibility to make judgment calls and decisions quickly and prudently**. In the days of our parents, executives could attain something akin to tenure and could rest comfortably in their seat of power until reaching retirement. Those days are gone. We know now that almost all roles in companies are performance-based at some level, and the folks at the top have wider and wider scopes of responsibility and are under intense pressure to deliver results. Add to that, in our twenty-four-seven, digitally connected world, most executives are never off the clock. **So your job is to synthesize the key elements of what the Hero needs to know to make a call—to decide—and to move forward.**

Imagine this. You're delivering a presentation that will decide whether a project you care about will go forward or not. You've got one shot.[6] The leadership team—the deciders—is gathered and attentive, but doesn't have the benefit of knowing what you know. The team doesn't understand the complexities and nuances of what you're bringing to the table. You're an expert on the topic. You've immersed yourself in the data, thought through the countless scenarios, and are confident in the right course of action. All you need the team to do is say "Yes." And so you begin.

Sadly, there's a massive difference between being an expert on a topic and being an expert at preparing a high-stakes presentation. **Subject matter expertise often introduces confusion rather than clarity.** In the book *Made To Stick,* by Chip and Dan Heath, they call this **the curse of knowledge**.

You've seen it a thousand times, I'm sure—slides packed to the margins with bullets and mind-boggling charts and graphs. And though all those charts and graphs may say something about one's ability to access data (which anyone can do), what it also says is that the presenters haven't done the work of distilling that data into its essential takeaways or answered the one key question.

---

[6] Cue Eminem's "Lose Yourself" playing in the background. *You only get one shot; do not miss your chance to blow. This opportunity comes once in a lifetime, yo!*

Actionable Plans to Drive Customer Acquisition

Go to Market Strategies and Tactics for Lead Generation
- PR Resource
  - Speaker at sections at Legal and relevant tech conferences
    - use BOA as leverage to get on the agenda
  - Articles for trade publications
    - Articles such as ABA Journal (June 2014 written by Alan Nathanson)
  - New Client acquisition releases
- Hone in on specific vertical targets (ie: Pharma-GSK, Media, Logistics Companies, Technology
  - Specific data driven forward thinking companies:
    - Netflix, IBM, Nielsen
- Produce Video to link to Align Matters website, Linked In, BOA communications, Cold Calls
- Identify and engage with evangelists
- Develop email list for Monthly-Weekly-Daily featuring Align updates and relevant content
- Provide BOA support materials for communication (sample RO Letter)
- Create a custom Align Video (60-90 seconds)
  - Explanation of the Align eco-system
- Consistent short and punchy communications focusing on the legal industry - data driven
- Create webinars
- Go to creative representative agencies CAA, WME, ICM, Paradigm
  - Pitch Align as a resource and talent agency representation for Align Brand and marketing partnerships

What Is the Quest and the Question at the Heart of It?

I love *The Matrix.* And it's not surprising that it follows the path of the universal Hero's Journey. But it also illustrates that a question is at the heart of every Hero's quest. In fact, both the word *question* and *quest* were derived from *quaerere*, meaning "to seek, ask, demand, or require." When Neo (the Hero) meets Trinity (the person who delivers the call to adventure), here's what she says.

It's the question that drives us, Neo. It's the question that brought you here. You know the question. Just as I did.[7]

Every quest starts out as a call to adventure, which will necessarily have trials and obstacles that must be overcome. It may feel silly at first to think of your job as a quest, but if you have goals, you have a quest. And at the center of that quest is a key question you must answer.

---

[7] Wachowski, Lana, and Lilly Wachowski. *The Matrix.* Warner Bros., 1999.

Let's look at the purpose of the quest itself. Every Hero has a goal, whether that's leading a company to greater profits or performing a task on a factory line without error. **What is your Hero's goal?** What is the treasure the person seeks? **What would make the person you're preparing this presentation for a Hero in their world?** Once you've identified that ultimate prize, you're entering the mind of the Hero and can start to ask questions.

In *The Matrix,* Neo asked, "What is the Matrix?" In the movie *Inception* (which we'll look at more closely in chapter 4), Leonardo DiCaprio's character asked, "Is this a dream?" In a sense, both Heroes were trying to solve a fundamental problem of their existence that would enable them to choose how to move forward. Your Hero also has a question they have to answer, and you are there to help them answer it. But which question?

Cisco's Novel Way of Setting up Companies

Bruce Botto, an internal consultant at Cisco, was tasked by his boss with figuring out how Cisco could set up dozens of legal business entities in foreign countries quickly and efficiently. It was something many other smart people at Cisco had tried and failed to figure out. Cisco was shifting its strategy from delivering services through business partners in foreign countries to delivering as Cisco Systems worldwide. Billions of dollars were at stake.

Many at Cisco had struggled to solve the puzzle. In fact, they had already spent tens of millions of dollars and multiple years trying to get these entities set up, unsuccessfully. At the time, they needed to set up about forty entities, and Botto recalled his boss's frustration: *"This can't take two or three years each and cost $15 million every time we do it. This is crazy. Why is it taking so long?"* Lucky for Botto,

he had been trained by Barbara Minto, the woman responsible for training associates at McKinsey on how to structure and produce written communications on complex subjects. Using Minto's method, which starts with **identifying the right question**, Botto accomplished what many others could not. *Why was it taking so long?*

As it turned out, the reason it was taking so long was a matter of Cisco's internal culture and closely held beliefs around finance and accounting principles. The roadblock to getting those entities set up came down to the process preferences of Cisco's own accountants. When I asked Bruce why others hadn't figured this out, he gave a simple piece of advice: ***Understand your audience. Understand the question they want answered.***

27

So, What Question Are You Trying to Answer for Your Hero?

Depending on who your WHO is, there are seven key questions your Hero could be asking. Here are a few thought starters, though this is by no means an exhaustive list.

The 7 Key Questions

WHAT (and which) questions

- ▶ What's the status?
- ▶ What is the problem?
- ▶ What is the opportunity? Which is best?

- ▶ What should we do?
- ▶ What are the stakes?

WHO

- ▶ Who do we need (employees, suppliers, customers, partners)?
- ▶ Who do we need to keep an eye on (competitors, collaborators)?
- ▶ Who else could affect the outcome?

WHEN

- ▶ When should we make a move?
- ▶ When will this be complete?
- ▶ When are the milestones?
- ▶ How long will this take?

WHERE

- ▶ Where is the problem, the opportunity, or the risk?
- ▶ Where should we market and sell?
- ▶ Where to next?
- ▶ Where should we expand (or contract)?

WHY

- ▶ Why does this matter?
- ▶ Why is this an opportunity or a problem?
- ▶ Why now?

HOW

- ▶ How do we get it done?
- ▶ How can we do it differently?
- ▶ How can we differentiate?

HOW MUCH/HOW BIG/ HOW SMALL

- ▶ How much will this cost? (business case, investment, or capital request)
- ▶ How big is the problem?
- ▶ How small can we make it?

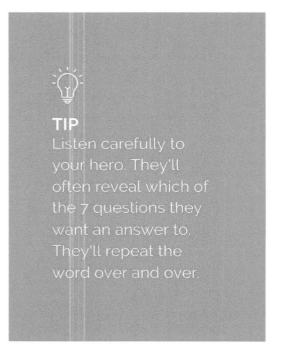

TIP
Listen carefully to your hero. They'll often reveal which of the 7 questions they want an answer to. They'll repeat the word over and over.

If you can identify the key question, you will understand your Hero's quest and thus will have the person's attention. After that, you just have to keep it by getting to the point. We'll cover that in the next chapter. But first, you need to align your agenda with your Hero's agenda.

Align Your Agendas

It would be foolish not to acknowledge that you also have skin in the game. You're trying to make something happen that either you yourself believe needs to be done or that you've been assigned to get done. Maybe it's a project you lead, a budget you need, or a resource you seek, but regardless of what it is, you need to influence this executive—this Hero—to arrive at the same conclusion that you've come to. The trick is to get them there more quickly and with less direct information than you had. **A good presentation gets to the point, builds authority, and instills confidence in your Hero (and your presentation's wider audience) so they can make a decision.**

To do this, you have to align your two objectives—yours and your Hero's. You'll need to show how your conclusion aligns to the quest they are on and the outcome that they need to get to in order to move their story forward.

Deckonomics™

A Health Care Example

When I worked with a big health care company on the West Coast, I learned the value of what's known as "retention" in marketing-speak. For a health care business, it's hugely important to keep members once they've been acquired (especially if they're healthy). This retention metric is always on the chief marketing officer's (CMO) performance dashboard among other key metrics such as membership growth. But both retention and growth programs compete for finite funding budgets. So the CMO has to decide where her dollars will get the best bang for her buck.

One of the projects I worked on was how to make the experience of visiting the medical centers more appealing and distinctive. Our hypothesis was that if we invested in designing and implementing a uniquely consistent "healing vibe" at our medical centers, then members would come to favor and expect it and would not settle for anything less. Thus, we'd keep members for longer.

Now, if you think about that from the CMO's perspective, that's an enormous commitment. It would take a lot of money, a lot of time, and perhaps even more challenging, a lot of evangelism with people in the company who have the "if it isn't broke, don't fix it" mentality. So you can imagine some of the questions that the CMO might have.

▶ How long will this take?
▶ How much will it cost?
▶ Has anyone else done this?
▶ How do we know it will work?
▶ How much longer would we expect our members to stay with us if we do it?
▶ Couldn't our competitors copy us?
▶ Etc.

The point is, it's hard to get people to cross the threshold, because there are always risks of failure. So what you need to do in your presentation is not only answer all of the obvious questions, but answer the ultimate question: Is this project worth it among all the other things the CMO could do with the company's resources?

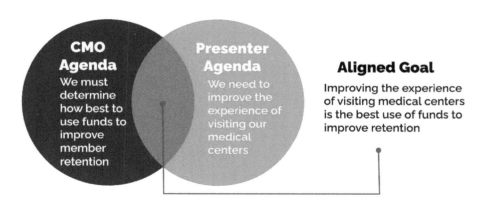

CMO Agenda
We must determine how best to use funds to improve member retention

Presenter Agenda
We need to improve the experience of visiting our medical centers

Aligned Goal
Improving the experience of visiting medical centers is the best use of funds to improve retention

That was my task—to develop a project that was both a good thing to do and a good use of funds relative to how those funds could have otherwise been used.

The Cisco Story, Part 2

Bruce Botto at Cisco accomplished what many in his place would not have accomplished because he identified the key question. In fact, as he pulled his findings into his presentation, he realized he would have to deliver an inconvenient message: *the enemy is us*. He went looking for a dragon to slay, and instead he found internal sacred cows that needed to be sacrificed instead. When I asked him how he managed what others didn't, here's what he said.

"

I set it up as two presentations that answered two different questions. In the first one, I said, "Other companies around the globe do this all the time. Do you want to know why we haven't been able to get this done?" When they said yes, I told them we had an internal problem and went through why we kept running into problems. That was the first presentation. At the end of that presentation, I asked another question. "Do you want to know the answer even if it means you're going to hear something that is going to violate certain points of view or strongly held beliefs by internal parts of the business, which—if we're willing to alter how we handle certain policies, processes, systems, and tools—will be absolutely possible?

"

When he got his yes to that question, Botto knew exactly what he needed to build for his second presentation. And that proposal was approved. Botto achieved with two presentations what many had died on the hill trying to do. He was able to do it because he was very clear about his Hero, the quest, and the question that he was there to help them answer.

Key Takeaways & Homework

▶ Identify the primary Hero and then adopt that person's mindset.

▶ Review the 7 Questions and brainstorm the answers from your Hero's point of view.

▶ Discover the Hero's quest and the key question at the heart of it.

▶ Align your agendas

Once you're clear on the Hero, the quest, and the key question you need to answer, it's time to aggregate and structure your content, and that's what we'll address in the next chapter.

Chapter 3
Create Structure

To communicate and persuade a decision-maker, you need to be an authority. Use the frameworks in this chapter to **tame the beast of information overload** and understand the problem to be solved.

Clear thinking is what separates pros from amateurs. Now that you've homed in on your Hero and their quest, it's time to get your thoughts in order. The process laid out in this chapter is going to help you do that.

The Curse of Knowledge

Recently, I was chatting with a client about what she wanted to accomplish in a presentation workshop with her team. I was curious why she thought they needed intensive training on building presentations. She told me how busy her team was and said that having to sit through presentations that meandered and didn't get to the point was a colossal drain and time waster. But an even bigger concern of hers was the image her team was projecting to the c-suite. She told me the story of a strategist in her company that we'll call Eve. She described Eve as "the smartest brain you could ever meet,

but for the life of her, she cannot present" and went on to describe the weird juxtaposition of Eve's brilliance versus her disconnected presentations.

We've all had the experience of sitting in a presentation and wondering, *"Where is this going?"* The reason is usually because the presentation simply hasn't been structured in the right way. A common mistake of many slide authors is to "write to think," and because the place they do the writing is PowerPoint, they confuse their slides full of words and bullet points with a presentation that's ready to go.

But being on the other side of this type of presentation is agonizing for the audience. It's like watching the presenter wrestle with the beast of the material in search of a conclusion. You see this often when a domain expert has what we call *"the curse of knowledge."* The domain expert knows so much about the topic and has connected so many ideas together, the person feels compelled to contain them all in one PowerPoint deck. But here's what's happening inside the mind of the audience:

The audience is getting fact after fact, anecdote after anecdote, but doesn't know where the story is headed. And because **the human brain is hard-wired to make meaning**, the audience inserts connective tissue to hold all the facts together in an attempt to predict the conclusion in their own minds. In other words, they weave their own storyline together. Here's the problem. If the audience's newly conceived story doesn't line up to the one you're presenting, you've lost them.

The presenter wrestles with the beast of the material in search of a conclusion. You see this often when a domain expert has what we call *'the curse of knowledge.'*

The domain expert knows so much about the topic, and has connected so many ideas together, **they feel compelled to contain them all in one PowerPoint deck**

The audience is getting fact after fact, anecdote after anecdote, but doesn't know where the story is headed. And because **the human brain is hard-wired to make meaning**, your audience inserts connective tissue to hold all the facts together in an attempt to predict the conclusion in their own minds

They weave their own storyline together. Here's the problem. If the audience's newly conceived story doesn't line up to the one you're presenting, you've lost them.

This *"everything and the kitchen sink"* approach to presenting a deck wastes everyone's time, leaves a terrible impression, and usually results in sending the slide author back to the drawing board, or worse, a flat-out rejection of your recommendation. Here's how to fix that right out of the gate.

Start with the Conclusion. What's the Point?

It's critically important that you **separate your thinking process from your writing process.** When you're giving your presentation, state the conclusion first, and then support your conclusion with a minimum of three logical supports or *proof points*. Of course, this presumes you already know what the conclusion is. In reality, it's rarely obvious at the beginning of the process. So let's look at how you might get to the conclusion.

Depending on how well you know the material, **there are two ways to proceed: 1) from the top down, or 2) from the bottom up.** The fastest way is top down, but for this approach you should know your material extremely well and anticipate that your audience will agree with your conclusion. If you're like most people, or are dealing with a complex topic, I urge you to work from the bottom up. You need to get all the data, the anecdotes, and the musings that are swimming around in your head, out into the clear light of day. That said, if you're forging ahead with the top-down approach, skip ahead to the *Presentation Brief* section in this chapter.

To test how well you know the point of the presentation, try expressing your point declaratively. For example, contrast these bad and good examples.

This is NOT the point of the presentation	This IS the point of the presentation
Discuss whether it's a good idea to enter the China market.	We should partner with Acme to enter the China market.
To propose options for increasing retention.	We need to establish 4 onboarding milestones that should increase long-term retention by 47%.
To share our progress on Project X.	We're informing the team that Project X fundraising has slowed and proposing new funding strategies.

If you're confident you know the point—the conclusion—then write that down on a sticky note as a complete sentence and put it in a prominent place wherever you're doing your thinking. Do not open up your slideware yet. We'll come back to that.

The next thing you need to do is logically support your point. Have you ever had the experience where you've been so deep into a topic and you have so much information swirling around in your brain that what seemed fairly straightforward at the start of the process has slowly but certainly turned into a jumble? Suddenly you realize that your mind has become the equivalent of Pandora's Box, and the thought of opening it makes you want to take a long nap.

At my company, we use at least two of three brainstorming tools on every slide deck we put together. The key to all of these tools is that they're tactile—you are interacting with your thought processes in a way that simply isn't possible by typing—and they activate different parts of your brain than would be activated by typing into your slideware. Why is that important? Well, without going into all the science, **the more you're in motion, the better your brain works.** It's why many of the smartest folks you've ever heard of (Einstein, Darwin, Thoreau, Taleb, Jobs) claimed to do their best thinking while taking walks.

The three brainstorming tools are:

Dump, Clump & Pyramid

For our money, **there's no better way to get all the ideas out of your head than to dump them onto sticky notes with a heavy marker.** They are fast, portable, and inexpensive. You don't need anything fancy, just a big stack of sticky notes and a surface (a wall, a window, a whiteboard, or even a large notebook will do). The dump and clump exercise is an absolute must if you're working in a team, because it allows everyone to get their ideas out.

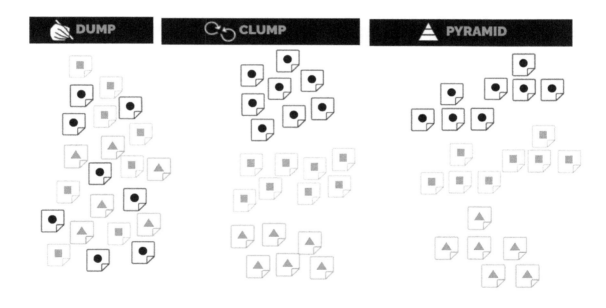

To demonstrate how to Dump, Clump, & Pyramid, we'll use the example of Project X. Project X is Jane and John's audacious plan to launch a mission to Mars.

Dump

The dump is all about getting all the disconnected ideas out of your brain and onto paper. Just start writing one idea per sticky note and set them aside, creating a stack as you go along. Resist the instinct to organize as you go. Go quickly and in whatever order the ideas come to you. It's important not to edit at this stage, so arm yourself with double the amount of stickies that you think you'll need. Regardless of what your presentation is about, there will be key things you need to capture. If it helps, you can use these prompts:

People

▶ Who are the people that populate this story?
▶ What are the roles, or departments, or groups of people involved?
▶ How are they structured?
▶ Are new skills needed?
▶ Is new capacity needed?

Place

► Are there specific geographic locations involved?
► Are there different functional areas?
► Where are all the players or systems, etc.?

Processes & Systems

► What's involved or needed in terms of systems, governance, or workflows?
► What are the steps involved in getting from Point A to Point B?
► What policies or protocols are working?
► What obstacles are stalling the work?

Technology

► Is there specific hardware or software needed? Other tools?
► How do different pieces of hardware and software connect?

Culture & Values

► What are the values that drive the business?
► What cultural norms are needed? Which of those need to change?

Metrics, Measures, & Motivators

► How will you measure progress?
► What are the ultimate indicators of success?
► What might be early indicators of success or failure?

Examples & Anecdotes

► Are there any stories, use cases, or testimonials that might support your conclusions?

These prompts are by no means exhaustive, but they should help get the wheels turning. Get everything you can onto a sticky note and don't worry about being organized. Also, give yourself plenty of time. It's really important for you to go past all the initial ideas. Push yourself. A standard pad of three-by-three stickies has a hundred sheets. Why not give yourself a challenge of filling an entire pad in thirty minutes? You'll notice you go really fast for the first twenty and slow down significantly when you pass fifty. But stickies fifty-one to one hundred will start to unfurl some real insights. Also, don't be afraid to throw in a few diagrams or drawings if that's the way you naturally think.

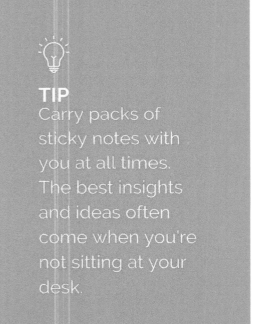

TIP
Carry packs of sticky notes with you at all times. The best insights and ideas often come when you're not sitting at your desk.

Oh, and here's another thing: **WRITE COMPLETE SENTENCES**, or as close to complete sentences as makes sense. I hate it when I look at a sticky note a few days later and wonder, *"What the hell was I thinking here?"* Having a sticky note that says *"collaborative features get rid of the blame game"* will be a lot more helpful when you're structuring your slides than a note that simply says *"blame game."*

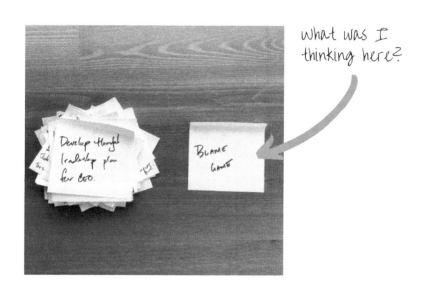

Some of you will be tempted to over-organize here—using different-colored stickies or different-colored markers to categorize thoughts as you go. The more complexity you add here, the higher the likelihood that you will get caught up in the logistics of brainstorming instead of just letting your thoughts flow. **Here's a tip** (you will thank me later): get plain yellow three-by-three stickies and a heavy black Sharpie.

Clump

Once you've got all of that information dumped onto sticky notes, you can now consciously clump it into order or patterns. **Our brains are wired to recognize patterns.** It's one of the biggest problem-solving tools we have. It allows us to anticipate danger, recognize familiar faces, order things along a spectrum, and even recognize the rhythm in tunes. This process of pattern recognition happens so fast in the brain that we don't always consciously know why we draw the conclusions that we draw. That's one reason that doing the brain dump is so important.

The other benefit of dumping all of your ideas, data points, hypotheses, and curiosities onto stickies is that you can clump them up on a wall and sort them into visual groups, which is something the brain is very good at. This clumping process will go quickly if you're working alone, but what if you're working with a group on your deck?

If you're working in a group, start putting all of your sticky notes on a wall together, *but silently*.

Here are the only rules to this exercise:

1. Put your stickies on a wall WITH the other members of the group. (i.e., each person is working on a single collective clumping exercise, intermingling their stickies with their teammates' stickies).

2. **Do it in complete silence.**

3. Keep going until every individual is satisfied with the entire arrangement. (That means that folks can move other people's stickies around if it serves the pattern they are recognizing.)

The goal of the exercise is for the group to collaboratively agree on a final grouping without ever verbally rationalizing what they're doing and why. **Something magical happens when you eliminate verbal language in a group clumping exercise.** For one, eliminating conversation ensures that the most persuasive talker doesn't govern the sorting and grouping of ideas. The other benefit of doing the exercise silently is that you get to observe how the others are making connections and recognizing patterns differently than you are. No matter how many times I've led this activity in workshops, participants are surprised and delighted at the insights they gleaned from the recipe of participation, observation, and silence. It's the ultimate example of *"mastermind"*

Clumping patterns can take four general forms.

1. **Sequential patterns** put things into an ordered sequence along some kind of dimension or spectrum (large to small, hot to cold, etc.).
2. **Chronological patterns** order things along a timeline.
3. **Priority patterns** rank things, for example, from most important to least important (this involves drawing conclusions from patterns).
4. **Relational groupings** are patterns built by association. For example, all things having to do with the software you need to complete a project would be a process of grouping parts that make up a whole. Separating software-related things from hardware-related things would be dividing a whole into different parts.

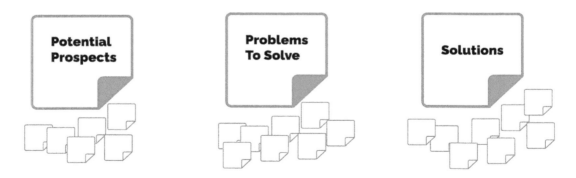

Now stand back. What do you see? Is there a way to draw conclusions from the groupings you have on the wall? If you had to turn each clump of sticky notes into a statement, what would that be? And most importantly, what is the highest-level statement you would want to make about the entire arrangement? Those statements are going to end up being the basis of your slide headers.

For example, if you were clumping the Project X plan to launch a mission to Mars, the following high-level statements could be a few of the things you'd address:

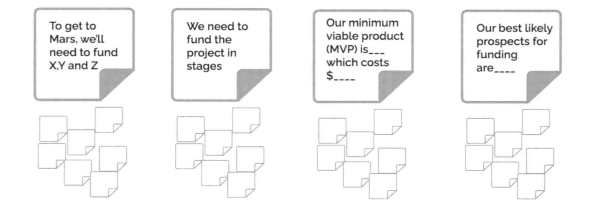

If you didn't already know the point of your presentation before you started, you should be able to draw a conclusion about what the point is now and have a handful of *proof points* to support your conclusion. In the same way that you need at least three legs to hold up a stool, you need to have at least three supports to hold up any believable conclusion. And that brings us to a subcategory of clumping, the Rule of 3s.

Belief and the Rule Of 3s

When law students learn to make an "argument," which is what you're doing with your conclusion, they learn that **for an argument to be "good," it must conform to the following three criteria:**

1. **The premises are plausible.** That is, there must be a good reason to believe that the premises are true.

2. **The argument must be valid or strong.**

3. **The premises are *more plausible* than the conclusion.**

Arguments need claims, reasons, and evidence in order to be believable. I want you to encode this in your memory: **your purpose in designing and delivering a presentation is to create belief!**

In order to create belief, though, **first you have to create an instance of uncertainty or questioning.** That's why you need a big bold statement. When you make your statement (your argument), your Hero must ask themselves, *"Do I agree or do I disagree? Or am I not sure?"* That's what puts them into a state of uncertainty and thus opens the window for you to guide them by laying out your support points and inviting the Hero into the mental journey of finding out what they believe.

How you sequence and support your argument will determine whether the audience agrees with you at the end of your presentation.

Don't believe me? There's all sorts of evidence of this in brainwashing. Whether you're investigating Chinese thought camps or religious cults, one thing you'll find over and over again is that besides isolating the individual whose beliefs you intend to change, you also need to introduce uncertainty. And, while we're not suggesting that you try to brainwash your Hero into agreeing with you, it is important for you to understand *why* encouraging the questioning mind is so important to building the conditions for persuasion before you introduce your logical supports.

If you don't create uncertainty (or at least draw attention to it), the mind will not be open to what you have to say. Uncertainty creates emotion, and that's why the best stories hook you and don't let you go. *Will Luke Skywalker find Princess Leia? Will Katniss Everdeen survive the Hunger Games?* **When people consume a story with a classic Hero's Journey, they want to know what happens next because the author has set the conditions for them to care.** But creating uncertainty alone is not enough for persuasion. The information you bring to the table (your premises) must be plausible, valid, and hard to argue with.

Think about all the threes you already know.

You started out with your ABCs and 123s.	An area code is three digits because its memorable.	You know about life, liberty, and the pursuit of happiness.	Steve Jobs notoriously used groupings of threes when he presented.	There were three wise men.
The Father, Son, and Holy Spirit.	Good, bad, and ugly.	Good, fast, and cheap.	The three musketeers.	Three legs on a stool.

Aristotle even used three in his book *Rhetoric*, the original book on persuasion, where he put forth that in order to persuade, you need three things: 1) credibility (ethos), 2) emotion (pathos), and 3) patterns of reasoning (logos).

Put simply, things in three are easy to remember. And, if you supply three supports to an argument and those supports are plausible, valid, and ideally, hard to argue with—you have a much higher likelihood of creating belief in your claim. Here's the bumper sticker: **Attach three sturdy legs beneath the stool of your argument and it will stand. Attach even more, and it may stand forever.**

Minto's Pyramid

At this point, you've dumped and clumped and have all the raw materials to build a strong structure. Now it's time to stress test it, and this is where Barbara Minto enters the picture. Barbara Minto was a consultant at McKinsey when she developed the Pyramid Principle to help their consultants write better reports for clients. She said, *"The pyramid is a tool to help you find out what you think. The great value of the technique is that it forces you to pull out of your head information that you weren't aware was there and then helps you to develop and shape it until the thinking is crystal clear."*

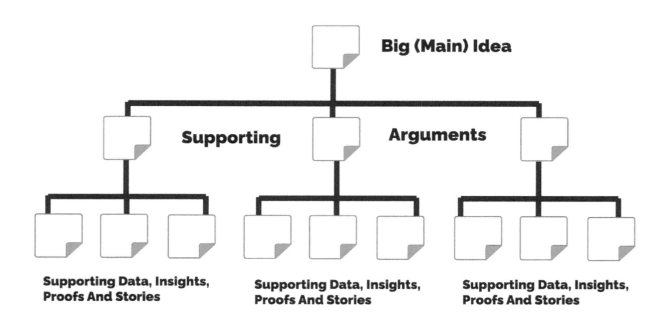

Big (Main) Idea

Supporting Arguments

Supporting Data, Insights, Proofs And Stories

Supporting Data, Insights, Proofs And Stories

Supporting Data, Insights, Proofs And Stories

The idea is to have your big idea derived directly from the supporting arguments and then derive those supporting arguments from the supporting data or evidence. Sound familiar? It's the Rule of 3s in the shape of a pyramid. Further, t**o create a logical pyramid, it must obey three rules.** (There are those threes again!)

1. The top of any piece of the pyramid needs to be a summary of the points below it.

2. The ideas or points in each grouping of the pyramid (usually a group of three) should all be *the same kind of idea.*

3. The ideas or points in each grouping must also be ordered logically. This is where those patterns you learned about in the last section come in.

For one of those patterns—the relational groupings—there's something else. In order to properly divide a whole into parts, those parts must be **mutually exclusive and collectively exhaustive.** We can credit Aristotle with the original concept, but Minto coined the term MECE (Mutually Exclusive, Collectively Exhaustive—pronounced appropriately like Greece). Meaning, once you finish your clumping exercise, all of your sticky notes will fit into groupings that don't overlap (making them mutually exclusive) and that also completely support your conclusion (making them collectively exhaustive).

As you inspect your groupings, how could you organize them into a pyramid? Examine your groupings and determine if the primary supports of your big idea are a group of causes and effects, a rank order, or a group of parts that make up a whole.

For example:

Cause and effects, sequential groupings.	In order to launch Project X, we have to secure funding. To do that, we must: 1. Create the project plan. 2. Build an estimate of total costs expected to support the plan. 3. Present the business case to the board for approval.
Rank order groupings	In order to launch Project X, we must solve a set of problems around the funding. • The biggest problem is that we're entering a period of cost-cutting across the enterprise. • Given the cost-cutting, we've got another problem -- Project X will have to compete with other important projects for funds. • And finally, the scope of this project doesn't fit neatly into any one department's budget.
Structural parts of a whole groupings	In order to launch Project X, we must form a team that can inform the business case. The team will need to include reps from: • Sales • Marketing • IT • Operations • Finance

If you already know the point of your presentation, it should be a relatively straightforward exercise to determine the type of logical grouping you'll need in order to support your big idea. If you don't yet know the point of your presentation, organizing your thoughts into a pyramid will probably point the big idea out to you.

Doodling for Deeper Insights

Are you ready to test your understanding? Behold the power of the doodle. **Doodles challenge your understanding and reveal connections.** We leverage doodling to expand our insights on almost every slide project we work on.

Specifically, we doodle different answers to the seven key questions you saw in the last chapter. Dan Roam wrote a brilliant little book called *Draw To Win* that encourages people to embrace drawing as a thinking exercise rather than an artistic one. And when you think about it, it makes a lot of sense. We've been drawing as a way of communicating ideas since before we developed a spoken language. Visual communication preceded verbal communication.

How powerful is a doodle? Southwest Airlines was famously conceived when two guys drew a triangle on a napkin at a bar in San Antonio.[8] That drawing is so central to their story that they have it featured on the history section of their website.

---

[6] I'm from San Antonio originally, so I love this story. In my imagination, they were at the Cadillac Bar, which I hope is still there as you read this.

Doodles capture concepts that are challenging to express in words, but at the same time make a concept stunningly clear. Even Einstein said that if he couldn't picture it, he couldn't understand it.

But before we go any further, I'm going to help you vanquish the idea that you can't draw. Anyone can *doodle*. Doodling just involves using shapes to illustrate a concept in the same way one simple triangle represented the first routes that Southwest Airlines would take. Roam points out that there are seven basic doodle shapes.

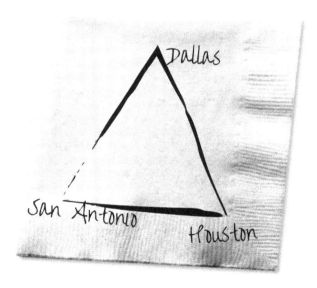

1. Dot
2. Line
3. Arrow
4. Square
5. Triangle
6. Circle
7. Blob

You'll use those seven shapes to create sketches that answer the seven questions of Why, Who, What, When, Where, How, and How Much—but we'll rearrange those questions to parallel how vision actually works. Close your eyes, take a beat, and then open them. **Now look at the picture below. What do you see?**

The first thing you'll notice is that you're taking a sort of spatial inventory.

1. You'll always gravitate to take in people or animals first. (WHO)

2. Then you'll note objects. (WHAT)

3. If there are patterns or groupings, you'll quickly take in how many. (HOW MUCH/MANY)

4. And you'll notice where they are spatially. (WHERE)

What did you see? Most people quickly identify three birds on a wire or a branch. But what else did you see? What did your mind infer from the data that your visual sense presented to your thinking brain? Though the drawing here is very simple, you likely told yourself a story about those three birds and drew some conclusions.

1. You noticed perhaps that this scene happens in the daytime, or when the birds are resting versus flying. (WHEN)

2. You may have noticed how they are arranged. There appears to be a smaller bird between two larger birds, and they are balanced on the wire. (HOW)

3. And finally, you may have concluded that the two larger birds are flanking the smaller bird because they are the parents of a baby bird. (WHY)

This sequence is always the same, and once you grasp that, you can **build stories in pictures that help you reveal the meaning behind all of that dumping and clumping you've done.**

Here's the other pretty cool thing. Each of those doodles answering the seven questions appeals to different roles in the organization.

Some people in the organization need to see the big picture. They're looking for context.

▶ **Functional leaders** and HR folks are concerned with one type of *Who*—the internal teams.

▶ **Sales and marketing folks** are concerned with another type of *Who* (the clients and customers) that comes into contact with the *What* (the product or service).

▶ **Chief financial officers** care about *How Many* (chart).

► **Strategy and operations folks** care about *Where* (map).

Other folks in the organization are concerned with the details.

► **Operations folks** want to know *When* (timeline) so they can get all their ducks in a row.

► **Operations, IT, and logistics folks** also want to know *How* (flowchart).

► And finally, **the CEO or functional leader** wants to know *Why* (conclusion)—why does the sum of all the other questions equate a competitive advantage?

Now let's put doodling to the test with Project X. In order for John and Jane to go to Mars, they're first going to have to raise funds to build and launch their rocket. How might we visually tell this story while answering the seven questions?

Notice below that in most cases, you will collapse the Who and What into a single frame, so though there are seven questions, we'll use just six doodles.

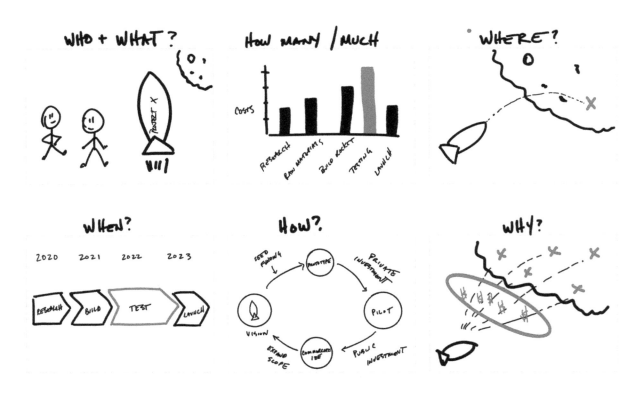

What story are the six slides telling here?

1. We start with Jane and John (*who*) and their visions of launching Project X (*what*).

2. Next, we have a graph telling us *how much* different components of the project will cost.

3. We've got a sense of *where* they want to go.

4. We've got a sense of *how long* it will take them to get to launch.

5. In the fifth panel, we see *how* they will go about funding the project.

6. And finally, we see *why* they want to launch Project X. Because if they can get to Mars once, they can probably get there many times.

Here's the other magical thing about doodling. **The act of doodling will help you better comprehend your content.** I can't tell you how many times we've sat down to doodle different answers to the questions and realized that we didn't know some of the answers (and thus needed to go find them), or didn't see a major insight sitting right in front of us. And the images, while simple, tell a visual story that can be grasped more directly than the same story could be told in words. If this story was told in words, the reader or listener would have to hold a multitude of ideas in active memory and string them all together with the reasoning brain to make sense. That's taxing and occupies mental resources from your audience that takes them out of the moment and steals critical attention away from your presentation.[9] But show them a visual, and you have direct access to the sensing brain. **Visuals are a shortcut to persuasion.**

I encourage you to create multiple versions of each of the doodle panels. The reason is that **as you sketch different doodle concepts, you will make new connections, gain new insights, and draw new conclusions.** Your doodles don't have to be artistic or even realistic; they just need to get the idea across to *you*. The bonus: when it's time for you to lay out your pages later, you'll also have an idea of the visual concepts to use on your slide. So grab a pad of sticky notes and doodle a few things. Use the template here, or download the template with prompts at www.deckonomics.com/resources.

---

[9] That's right. Your mental resources are finite, which is why analysis paralysis is real. Daniel Kahneman goes into this in fascinating detail in his book *Thinking Fast and Slow*.

6 SLIDE TYPES TO PERSUADE

WHO/WHAT (Portrait)
Qualitative representations (CMO)

HOW MUCH (Chart) Q
Quantitative representations (CFO)

WHERE (Map)
Position is space (CSO)

WHEN (Timeline)
Position in time (COO)

HOW (Flowchart)
Cause and effect (CTO)

WHY (Summary equation)
Deduction and prediction (CEO)

If you doubt the power of doodles, check out Dan Roam's health care presentation on Slideshare.[10] When the United States was trying to reform health care in 2008, the country divided against itself according to party lines with very different understandings of how health care worked. Roam and a doctor colleague put together a series of doodles to understand what was really going on. When they put their drawings into a PowerPoint with simple headlines and posted them online, their doodles ended up being downloaded over fifty thousand times within a month. In fact, those doodles explained things so clearly that Roam was invited to present them on national news and ultimately was invited to the White House, twice! Turns out that many people in government got their health care education from his set of doodles.

[10] https://www.slideshare.net/danroam/healthcare-napkins-all

Summary

You are now armed with a systematic way to organize your thoughts prior to a pitch. **Organizing your argument is the most important determinant of how successful your presentation will be.** When I think of Eve, the woman who knew too much, I think about the parallels that meditation has with slide authorship. In breath meditation, there's a concept of "thoughtless awareness" that exists between breaths. Actively and consciously focusing on your breath is one of the easiest ways to slow the mind down and push out the clutter and noise of incessant thought loops. But *it's the pause between the inhalation and exhalation where the good stuff is* — where nothing and everything coincide simultaneously.

The same is true for great presentations. **The data and facts and charts are not really what the presentation is about. Rather, it's the *insights* — the web of connections between all of those data points and the conclusions — that matter. That's where the gold lies.** Eve would have done better to share her *ahas* than share proof of her analysis. That's what you'll be able to do with the tools outlined in this chapter.

Key Takeaways & Homework

▶ To find the point of your presentation, start by dumping all of your ideas and data points onto sticky notes, and then clump them into groupings.

▶ Once you've clumped your sticky notes into groupings, put them into a hierarchical Minto pyramid.

▶ Discover new insights about your topic by using the seven core questions to draw six doodles.

Now that you know the point of your presentation, how you'll support your point in a way that creates belief, and you've been able to doodle your way to further insights . . . let's get your information into a quick and dirty brief that will serve as your GPS as you build out your slide presentation outline.

Chapter 4
Write Your
Presentation Brief

Use a presentation brief to **capture your high-level presentation on a single page.**

This is a presentation brief

BRIEF

TOPIC:

DATE:

VERSION:

MAIN POINT

SITUATION / CONTEXT

- What is the situation, or non-controversial statement that everyone will agree with? Why are you having this conversation?

KEY QUESTION / COMPLICATION

- What is the key question you are here to answer for your audience?

BIG IDEA

What statement contains the BIG IDEA, and has a clear point of view. Write this as a complete sentence.

SUPPORT POINT 1

SUPPORT POINT 2

SUPPORT POINT 3

RED FLAGS, REBUTTALS & RESISTANCE

What are the spoken and unspoken reasons your primary audience will resist your conclusion or avoid taking action?

CALL TO ACTION / CALL TO ARMS

What action do you want the audience to take now? Why now? What is the next step?

This framework is proprietary. ©2020, Zuzaeta Group

You can download the presentation brief worksheet with prompts at deckonomics.com/resources

When we work with clients to help develop presentations, we do presentation briefs for two reasons.

1. First, it helps us **see on a single page the full context of the argument we'll make, the obstacles or barriers we might encounter to our argument, and the request we'll make, whether explicit or implicit**. It's a stress test that will enable you to find out whether you have in fact arrived at a tight enough argument around which to structure your presentation.

2. The second reason we do the brief is that it's a great **calibration tool for teams or leadership when creating a high-stakes presentation. It allows you to validate your approach to the presentation and its logic with others prior to building out all the pages.**

Looking at the brief you'll see that the left two-thirds of the page is where we lay out the elements of the argument, and the right side is where we anticipate objections and articulate *"the ask."* The brief allows you to capture both the logic and the high-level story elements in one place.

Anatomy of a Presentation Brief

Panels 1 and 2 recap the context and the conflict. Put in storytelling terms, they recap the Hero's quest (to enter new markets that will represent a significant value to the company) and the question that leads to the promise (is there a viable way to accomplish this?), which is the point of the presentation. While these two items may not end up as slides in your presentation, they are the reason you're doing your presentation in the first place, so you need to jot them down. I can't tell you how often I see slide decks that never get around to answering the key question.

Panels 3 and 4a-c represent the meat of your argument, and you should be able to pull the work you did earlier on Minto's

pyramid directly into this section. If you didn't do that exercise as a lead-up to this brief, here's where you'll capture it now.

In **panel 3**, summarize your point as a bold claim in a clear and direct complete sentence. This is effectively the title of your story, and it needs to have a point of view.

Panels 4a, 4b, and 4c should simply be your support points that are logically ordered as a sequence, as a rank order, or as structural parts of the whole. Remember, if they are structural parts of a whole, they must be MECE (see above). How do you know which logical order you have?

- ► This, then this, then this, then everything else is a sequence.

- ► Most to least, best to worst, highest to lowest, nearest to farthest. These all represent *rank orders*.

- ► See, touch, hear, taste, and smell. These are *parts of a whole* that are the five senses.

The sweet spot is between three and seven support points, with few exceptions. With fewer than three, the argument won't feel sufficiently supported—you will leave room for doubt.

Over seven and the argument could feel convoluted and confusing, also introducing doubt. Also, note that your support points will probably need to be supported with data, insights, and conclusions that themselves are MECE. Arguments need logical conclusions, and conclusions are always MECE.

In panel 5, you should anticipate resistance and rebuttals. No matter how well you make your argument, your Hero as a human will create stories about the risks of taking action. Every Hero knows from experience that there will always be trials and setbacks. Regardless of whether you account for them, they *will* still form in your Hero's brain and they will formulate their own responses to those risks. You're better off anticipating them now and guiding how the Hero should respond to them.

And finally, in panel 6, you'll summarize your ask. You'll want to be extremely clear about what you are asking your Hero (and wider audience) to do. It's surprising how often presentation authors forget this. Even if you have a soft request, it's still important to know what you want from the audience when you're done. For example, say you're just trying to get buy-in on an idea. You might then ask for a show of hands on all who agree with your approach and then request they circulate a memo you've pre-written to inform their teams

about the work. Or you could do the opposite and ask if they see any reason not to proceed as you intend.

Look at an example here where I was prepping for a presentation with a financial services client. Here, some new research showed that there was an opportunity to serve a growing segment of high net-worth women. Our goal was to persuade the chairperson to release funds to create a training series for them, but also to commit to hiring more women advisors.

BRIEF

DATE:

VERSION:

MAIN POINT

SITUATION / CONTEXT

What is the situation, or not-so-obvious danger that keeps me up at night? Why are you raising this now/at all?

1. We want to expand our reach to serve more women.

———————————

KEY QUESTION / COMPLICATION

What is the key question you are here to answer for your audience?

2. But women are less likely to trust their skills in managing money.

———————————

BIG IDEA

What document contains the BIG IDEA and your unique point of view. Write this as a complete sentence.

3. We need to educate and empower women to feel confident managing their money with a training series.

SUPPORT POINT 1

4a. There's a rising wealth shift to women

SUPPORT POINT 2

4b. Women want to focus on real-life goals

SUPPORT POINT 3

4c. Women are likely to succeed w/ sound advice.

RED FLAGS, REBUTTALS & RESISTANCE

What are the red flags that might prevent your primary audience from taking your point of view or from taking action?

- There aren't as many high net worth women as men
- Women will be harder to target
- Women prefer someone who is personally recommended

CALL TO ACTION / CALL TO ARMS

What action do you want the audience to take now? Why now? What is the next step?

6. Let's build a training series just for high net worth women, and include influencers as speakers.

This framework is proprietary. ©2020, Zurawska Group

Guess what? This brief guided us to develop a presentation that got the chairperson across the threshold. We persuaded the client to develop an event targeted at high net-worth women based on our research that showed that a huge wealth transfer to women is underway, that women make investments for different reasons than men do, and that they are open to professional advice. Gathering and organizing our thoughts helped us overcome the curse of knowledge.

Summary

Completing a presentation brief before you go headlong into banging out a bunch of pages is a great way to keep your story tight and also to make sure you're telling the story your Hero wants to hear.

Key Takeaways & Homework

► Summarize your presentation approach in a brief to stress test your thinking.

► Use your brief to calibrate with others before you develop your slides.

Chapter 5
Building Your Storyboard for Persuasion

Design a persuasive presentation using **the 12Ps of the Persuasion Journey.**™

There's a great exchange that starts the movie *Inception* that gets to the root of what you, the presentation author, are really trying to do. In the movie, Cobb, played by Leonardo DiCaprio, explains to Mr. Saito, his client, one hazard of the subconscious mind—it's malleable. **The mind is open to suggestions.** He says, *"Once an idea has taken hold of the brain, it's almost impossible to eradicate. An idea that is fully formed—fully understood—that sticks."* [11]

Persuasion, when it is fully achieved, is transformational precisely because it plants an idea in your audience's brain that takes root and grows on its own.

[11] Nolan, C. (2010). *Inception*. Warner Bros.

Presentations Should Almost Always be Designed for Persuasion

You learned in the last chapter that whether you have an implicit or explicit *"ask,"* you are there to persuade your audience of something—whether it's to give you something, do something, or simply see things as you see them. The most direct route to getting your intended outcome is to do something akin to what Cobb does in *Inception*—plant an idea into someone else's subconscious. Now, before you get squeamish about this, understand that I am not suggesting you plant a manipulative idea in someone's mind. That will always catch up with you. But here's what the latest brain science says—**our brains are creating stories to construct our reality at all times.**

There's a brilliant book, *How Emotions Are Made – The Secret Life of the Brain* (Barrett, 2017), that explains how modern brain science has revealed that in much of our waking life we are running a simulation of what we expect reality to be.

The brain spends eternity in a dark, silent box. It cannot get out and enjoy the world's marvels directly . . . With only past experiences as a guide, your brain makes predictions [through which] it constructs the world you experience.

-- Elizabeth Barrett

This ability to run a simulation in anticipation of reality, and the fact that the anticipation comes directly from previous experiences, is one reason stories play such a profound role in persuasive presentations. Because, as you lead someone through a storyline, you are sending information into the black box called the brain in the same way that the *senses* do. **You are creating a fresh experience that the brain will add to its previous experiences, and *that*—pay attention to this—will affect future predictions and decisions.**

Think of it this way. Your brain is like an artificial intelligence (AI). The AI doesn't really know what reality is and isn't. You teach it by giving it information. You send information into the AI, and it runs simulations and spits out a prediction of the answer. How does it know whether the answer is right or wrong? It waits for negative feedback. It's the same reason the brain doesn't know it's dreaming until you wake up and tell it, *"That was a dream."*

And so, by creating a story, you're effectively taking the brain on a little journey that it will then tuck into its file of previous experiences so that when you make your ask at the end of the presentation, your Hero will already have run the simulation successfully without negative consequences. That will make it easier for them to say yes when you make your request.

---

[12] If you want to know more, check out Daniel Kahneman's *Thinking, Fast and Slow*.

Your Job Is to Change Minds. But Change Is Hard.

The reason the story format is so important is that it's the best tool we have for inducing a simulation. And the simulation aspect of the story is critical because we humans are mostly resistant to change. Why? Because change involves us venturing into the unknown. The aspect of our brains that is making constant predictions throws up a red flag each time we introduce change, warning us that it doesn't have enough information to run a simulation with high confidence.

The brain is biased toward having you do things it has already done and can predict with a high level of certainty.[12] So when you're in a situation where you need your audience to make a change, you're asking them to defy the safety of the past and leap into the unknown where the outcome is not so certain. And the brain responds with, "Well, wait a minute. I haven't had a chance to run this scenario yet. I don't have enough data to make an accurate prediction, so I better approach with caution."

The story format allows you to effectively run the simulation for your audience so that when you ultimately make your request, the brain has received some additional data and can lower its defenses. This is so important to persuasion! If you don't create a new simulation and show that what you're asking your Hero to do can actually be achieved without negative consequences, their brain will default to its "tried and true" state and resist taking action. It's the reason that ineffective presentations simply package up the same set of facts and data that the audience has already seen.

Adapting the Hero's Journey for Persuasion Creates the Right Conditions for Change.

As you've already seen, the Hero's Journey is a universal story that everyone can relate to in some fashion. But for our purposes, I want you to address a very specific part of that journey—the part that **leads the Hero from their ordinary world to take action and cross the threshold.**

Let's take another look at the first five milestones on the Hero's Journey with a quick example.

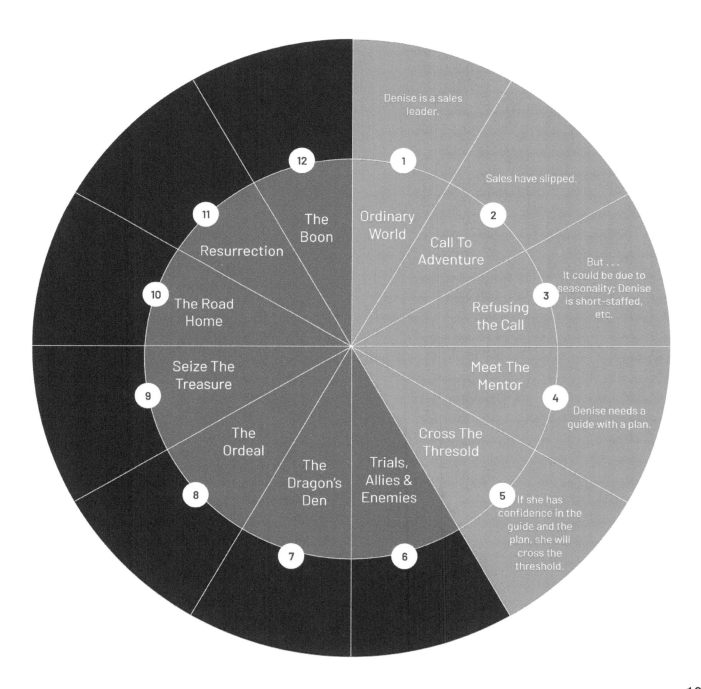

Denise is a sales leader.

Sales have slipped.

But . . .
It could be due to seasonality; Denise is short-staffed, etc.

Denise needs a guide with a plan.

If she has confidence in the guide and the plan, she will cross the threshold.

Ordinary World

Call To Adventure

Refusing the Call

Meet The Mentor

Cross The Thresold

Trials, Allies & Enemies

The Dragon's Den

The Ordeal

Seize The Treasure

The Road Home

Resurrection

The Boon

1. You start out with your Hero in her *ordinary world*. In this case, we have Denise who is a sales leader at a bank.

2. And then something happens where the Hero receives a *call to adventure*— in this case, maybe sales have slipped and Denise needs to do something about it.

3. Your Hero will initially *refuse the call*, even if only mentally. Perhaps Denise thinks to herself that the sales slip is temporary because of seasonality. Or she may, in fact, want to address the issue, but has so much on her plate already that she doesn't think she can solve the problem until she hires someone. Regardless, this is where her safety defenses come up. She'll think about all the dangers of doing something different. *For example, what if she makes a change and makes the situation worse?* Her instinct will be to ride it out. (Ultimately, the reason that taking decisive action is so hard for all of us is because we all wonder, "What if I'm making the *wrong* decision?") This instinct is so strong that we're going to really pay attention to it as we build the presentation.

4. Then *the mentor or guide appears*, and in this case that's you. Your job is to explain that everything's going to be okay because you've got a plan.

5. And finally, if you do a good job detailing your plan to your Hero, you will get Denise to *cross the threshold*.

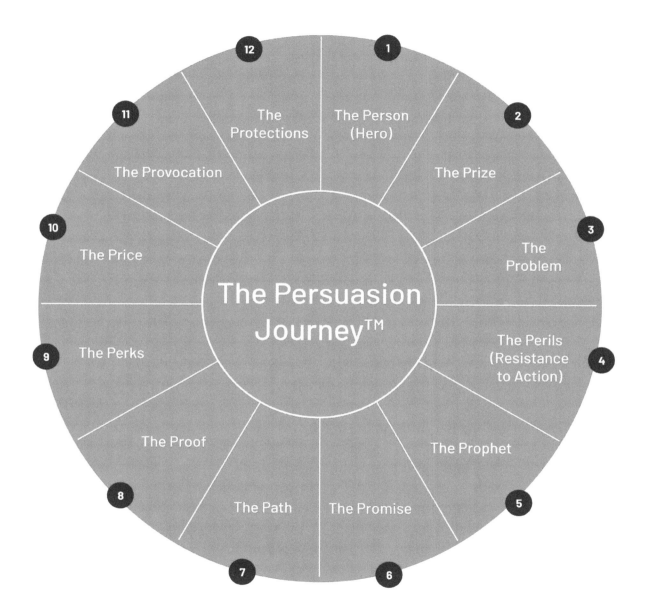

What you have so far is a little over the first third of the broad Hero's Journey cycle, and that's the part that you'll be mostly concerned with when you author a presentation. But, as you'll see, there is a complete cycle within that bigger journey that we call the *Hero's Persuasion Journey™*.

Building a Persuasion Journey with the 12 Ps

Let's revisit what you've already done, quickly. You've stress tested the logic of your argument with Minto's pyramid, and hopefully you've calibrated with your team that you are addressing the right question by creating a brief. Now it's time to look at the cycle within the cycle that we mentioned earlier—the Persuasion Journey™.

This is where you will construct a journey for your Hero that takes all the *think-work* you've done and packages it into a story (a simulation) so your Hero can assess and determine if they agree with you, but in a *shortened amount of time*—the time it takes you to make your presentation and then discuss it.

Remember Neo from *The Matrix?* His journey can't truly begin until he chooses (decides) to know the truth. He has to make that decision, knowing that his journey will not be easy. This isn't all that much different from what executives have to do daily in the workplace. They must decide to do the hard things that will move their company forward, and you are there to help guide the way.

So how can you help them? **The trick to getting your Hero to *"answer the call"* and to *"cross the threshold"* is to show them what lies on the other side of the threshold and give them the confidence that they can complete the journey successfully.** In effect, what you're doing is taking them to the threshold in *real life,* but helping them "simulate" the rest of the journey in their *minds* so they can make the right decision with confidence. You are planting the seed of an idea and creating the conditions for the seed to grow. **When you lead someone through a persuasion journey, what you're really trying to do is create a new confidently held belief.**

The 12 Ps of the Persuasion Journey™

Just as with the Hero's Journey, the Persuasion Journey™ also has twelve milestones but is geared toward helping your Hero simulate the journey they must take to claim their prize. Let's deconstruct a real business situation to examine how the Persuasion Journey™ works.

A few years back, I worked with a company that was considering upgrading its marketing automation software. Everyone hated the software the company had been using for the last ten years. It was clunky, buggy, and grossly limited in what it could do. The problem, though, was that it had been MacGyvered to such an extent by various departments in the company that it was going to be very hard to unwind and transition away from. The following case study is fictionalized but is very close to how we dealt with the problem.

Banka Case Study

Hank is a director at a large bank, Banka.[13] He wants to persuade his VP, Denise, to invest in new software (called Diletat) that will help the bank deliver more personalized communications to customers.

---

[13] Note, this example has been fictionalized to protect the innocent. While the situation is real, Banka is a fictional bank, and the characters and software companies have been fictionalized as well.

1. The Person (Hero) — Denise is dubious.
2. The Prize — She needs to increase usage of products.
3. The Problem — But she doesn't have great communications tools.
4. The Perils (Resistance to Action) — She's afraid she'll select the wrong tool.
5. The Prophet — Hank is a data expert.
6. The Promise — Hank has a way to increase product usage with a new tool.
7. The Path — The new tool will enable a better onboarding experience and personalized offers.
8. The Proof — Hank's data proves his hypothesis, and the tool is being used by other large companies.
9. Perceived Benefits — The tool will drive retention while lowering expenses.
10. The Price — The cost is $6.2 million to implement.
11. The Provocation — They can start with a pilot to prove the tool before scaling it.
12. The Protections — If they don't get results, they can cancel the contract.

107

The first part of the Persuasion Journey™ is all about demonstrating that you, the mentor, understand the Hero, their quest, and the obstacles to the quest. While P1 (the person) and P5 (the prophet) are critical, they don't necessarily need slides. That's not to say you don't need to give them your attention. To have a persuasive presentation, understanding the roles of the Hero and mentor is essential, but they rarely need to be specified, especially if your presentation is to an internal audience. You'll get your Hero's attention by showing that you understand them, their goal, and the obstacles to that goal in Ps 1–4 (person, prize, problem, perils), and that you are uniquely qualified to be their guide in P5 (prophet).

P1: Person
This is this the first of the often 'silent' P's — meaning you won't necessarily need a slide for this. Still, you must fix your Person (hero) very specifically in your mind in order to construct a persuasive deck. It's not enough to identify the primary person you will be appealing to, you also really need to understand their world and what's at stake from their point of view.

Denise, the VP, is dubious but open. While she believes more personalized communications will deliver a better experience to customers, she wonders if they will deliver an ROI of time and money. She's also concerned about the change management needed to implement the software. The investment needed for the software and training is substantial, and this project isn't the only one that is vying for limited funds.

P2: Prize
In order to appeal to Denise, Hank needs to hang his argument on a goal that Denise cares about.

One of Denise's big responsibilities is promoting new products to customers. It's one of the key metrics she is evaluated on. Hank believes more personalized communications will result in improved adoption of new products.

P3: Problem & Pain
Hank needs to introduce the problem and show how it gets in the way of Denise's end goal.

The problem is that the tool that Banka currently uses to send and track electronic communications (Commodo) is limited to just that — send and track. It doesn't integrate with other systems and processes the bank uses to interact with customers. Hence, they are missing opportunities to trigger timely and relevant communications when customers' interactions with the bank start to change.

Plus, Banka is losing customers when competitors advertise heavily. Hank has done some analysis and noticed that the customers they lose are also the most disconnected Banka customers - and specifically customers with the least number of accounts.

P4: Perils & Obstacles to action
Denise will always have a running narrative in her 'thought cloud' warning her of the things that could go wrong, so Hank needs to anticipate these.

From his experience with Denise, Hank thinks that Denise might be thinking the following:
- what if Diletat can't manage Banka's email volume?
- what if Diletat is too hard to use?
- what if Diltetat doesn't integrate well with other programs?
- what if the function of the program works, but it doesn't yield the results they're looking for from it?
- what if it costs so much and uses so many resources, it puts other key programs in peril?

P5: Prophet
Remember that even though this P is often silent, the Prophet must still be believable. Hank needs be an authority on the topic, or come to the table with authority in hand .

Hank is a data expert, and has discovered some key information that could improve uptake on new accounts.

You'll create a state of intrigue as they wonder whether they will agree with your bold statement in P6 (promise). In P7 (path) you'll simulate the future path they'll take, and they will see that what they want is indeed achievable, logical, and seems easy because you've given them the course of action that will lead to their desired outcome in a simple and easy-to-understand sequence. In P8 (proof) you'll supply substantial reasons to believe.

P6: Promise

Hank needs to make a bold claim that makes Denise and others want to pay attention.

Banka can increase overall accounts and accounts per person if they re-engineer their onboarding experience to get the customer to accomplish 3 key milestones that characterize connected customers: 1) register for paperless communications; 2) open and maintain a personal checking account; and 3) establish automatic bill-pay for at least 2 monthly bills. And Diletat can deliver on this capability.

P7: Path

Hank must break down how to accomplish the task with (ideally) 3 - 7 steps. Breaking down chunks of the path into a sequence of logical steps makes it easy for the audience to grasp what needs to be done. Complexity is the enemy of action.

With the new system from Diletat . . .

- When a new customer enrolls at a branch, the customer account will be flagged and enter the onboarding sequence that guides them to complete the 3 milestones.
- The **first milestone** will be to persuade the customer to sign up for paperless communications - this allows Banka to communicate with the customer more often, and in a more timely and cost efficient manner since they won't need to mail communications.
- **Milestone 2**: The customer will be urged to complete a transaction on their personalized concierge-style portal or mobile app — this will train them to do their banking online.
- **Milestone 3**: Customers will be incentivized to use Banka as their primary bill paying bank with free instant bill pay on the web or through the mobile app.

Subsequent offers will be made to the customer triggered by their specific interactions with the bank designed to increase utilization.

P8: Proof

Hank must show Denise that she is not stepping into uncharted waters. In fact, Banka has already walked the path, albeit without intention.

Also, notice that in P8 you start closing the loops you opened in P4 (Perils and Obstacles to Action). You must close all significant loops by the end of the deck.

Hank has data showing that customers who have accomplished the 3 key milestones shift their primary banking to Banka, and open more accounts.
Furthermore, Diletat is already providing services to several of the top 10 banks in the country, which eliminates any concerns about their ability to handle large volumes and integrate with complex systems.

Finally, you will "land the plane" in Ps 9–12 (perks, price, provocation, and protections) with your Hero understanding that they'd be nuts NOT to decide to take action.

P9: Perks

In direct marketing terms, we call this 'the stack'. Here Hank must show that the additional perks gained for purchasing the new Diletat software goes beyond adoption of new products. This is also where you continue to close loops that will impede action. This benefit stack needs to be explicitly stated, such that the price will be dwarfed by benefit.

Note the benefit doesn't always need to be quantifiable in financial terms, though it helps. The benefit could also be soft benefits.

- Customers who achieve the 3 milestones increase their switching costs, making them less likely to chase competitor offers.
- These customers tend to stay customers for 10 years or more, reducing overall churn.
- Reducing churn drives down the cost of re-acquisition.
- Digital communications delivery drives down the cost of paper communications.
- Customers who accomplish the 3 milestones will turn to Banka for further banking needs like mortgages, lines of credit, credit cards, etc.
- If Banka can increase the number of customers who achieve the 3 milestones by just 5%, a conservative goal, they will increase overall revenue by $160 million per year for the next 3 years.

P10: Price

By the time you get to the price, the investment should seem small.

Note, the price could also be 'soft', for example, it could be the time invested.

The cost of implementing the new system is only $6.2 million, and will only require a small team to implement.

P11: Provocation

This is where Hank needs to explicitly state what he needs to move things forward. Here it is signing a letter of intent. Urgency and scarcity will increase the likelihood of action.

Hank will ask for permission to move forward with a letter of intent. As an incentive, if Banka signs a letter of intent prior to year's end, Diletat is offering to run a pilot in the Sacramento region at break-even cost to prove that they can increase engagement with new customers.

P12: Protections

Even with a perfectly logical argument that has obvious benefits that outweigh the cost, your hero could be reluctant to stick their necks out in favor of change. That's why some form of risk-reversal protections should always be included.

Banka will only be obligated to follow through with the contract if Diletat achieves its goal of increasing engagement. If Diletat cannot achieve its goal, Diletat will assume all costs of migrating the Sacramento region back to Commodo.

This framework of the 12 Ps enables you to build a horizontal story that will move your Hero forward in their journey.

Your Horizontal Story

The 12 Ps give you a guide for your horizontal story. Now you need to return to your trusted sticky notes and write one sentence per P horizontally (noting that

P1 and P5 are often "silent" and don't need slides). These will be your "draft" headlines.

PERSON	PRIZE	PROBLEM	PERILS	PROPHET	PROMISE
Dubious Denise	We need customers to enroll for new products.	Our current tools don't enable personalization, and we're losing customers.	We need a solution that's easy to deploy and delivers an ROI.	Hank has the answer (he's a data expert).	We need a new onboarding experience (and the tech to drive it).

PATH	PROOF	PERKS	PRICE	PROVOKE	PROTECT
Implement Diletat, and guide new customers through 3 milestones for better retention.	Current customers that have crossed these milestones also use a wider range of products.	The new system will reduce churn and increase revenue. $$$	Diletat will cost $6.2M to implement, and then $800k/year	They're willing to run a pilot in Sacramento at cost if we sign an LOI by EOY.	If the pilot doesn't work, we can terminate the LOI.

In some contexts, ten slides for the ten Ps will be adequate for even the most complex presentation. And we could collapse them into fewer slides if needed. But the number of slides is not the most important thing, regardless of the limits your overlords have placed upon you. The most important thing is constructing a storyline that will guide your conversation persuasively. The horizontal story is the spine of your presentation. It enables your audience to follow the narrative that you're communicating in a sequence that feels right and reflects how we naturally assimilate and organize information.

TIP
If you're having trouble outlining the 12Ps on a deck you'll present in the future, try outlining the 12Ps on a presentation you've made in the past.

Your Vertical Story Legs

If you look closely, you'll also notice something else about the order of the Ps. Ps 1–6 are all about the conflict between the current reality and the desired reality. They highlight what the problem is. P7 is about how to get from current to future reality—it's the bridge to the desired reality. And Ps 8–12 are all the reasons now is the time to undertake the journey from current to future reality.

▶ P1–6 = What the problem is

▶ P7 = How to solve the problem

▶ P8–12 = Why to solve the problem, and why now.

Once you have the horizontal story sorted, which will give your presentation a sense of progression and pace, you'll use elements from your dump and clump exercise to fill in your vertical story.

PERSON	PRIZE	PROBLEM	PERILS	PROPHET	PROMISE
Dubious Denise	We need customers to enroll for new products.	Our current tools don't enable personalization, and we're losing customers.	We need a solution that's easy to deploy and delivers an ROI.	Hank has the answer (he's a data expert).	We need a new onboarding experience (and the tech to drive it).
		We don't account for customers current type of account(s).	Can we find a vendor who can handle our volume?		
		Don't consider usage of accounts.	What if the system doesn't integrate with other tech we have?		
		We don't account for how long we've had the customer.	The system has to be cost positive in 2 years.		

PATH	PROOF	PERKS	PRICE	PROVOKE	PROTECT
Implement Diletat, and guide new customers through 3 milestones for better retention.	Current customers that have crossed these milestones also use a wider range of products.	The new system will reduce churn and increase revenue. $$$	Diletat will cost $6.2M to implement, and then $800k/year	They're willing to run a pilot in Sacramento at cost if we sign an LOI by EOY.	If the pilot doesn't work, we can terminate the LOI.
1. New customers will get flagged for new onboarding program.	Engaged customers are 42% more likely to have a savings account.	Customers with more accounts stay 10 years or longer.		Pilot will allow us to baby-step our way in.	If pilot goes poorly, we can get out of the deal.
2. Customer will be encouraged to enroll in paperless communications.	...and 149% more likely to have a credit card.	Reducing churn will reduce marketing expense.		Will allow us to develop SOP's and design contained experiments.	Tight performance window minimizes resource impact.
3. Customer will gain access to personalized portal.	...and 232% more likely to have a mortgage with Banka.	We project $160mm increase in revenue per year.		Will enable us to benchmark Sacramento against other regions.	If pilot is unsuccessful, Diletat will revert back to current state at no cost.

The most important places to support your story are around the problem and the imagined perils to solving it. **If you think about stories, it's always the conflict that drives the story forward.** Neo wants to know the truth about the Matrix. Luke Skywalker wants to avenge his family in *Star Wars*. If you correctly identify the problem, shine a light on it, and expose the second-order consequences of the problem (the pain), you will stimulate a powerful need to resolve the problem. Ps 1–3 are about revealing the stark contrast between the current state and the desired state. **Contrasts are powerful emotional triggers,** and as you've learned in previous chapters, you need your Hero to get emotional in order to get them into action. But you'll also need them to conquer the fears you identified in P4.

Supporting the Problem and Perils

Here is where we'll return again to Minto's pyramid. For P3 and P4, think about evidence, anecdotes, and metaphors that will add weight to what you're saying.

For example, here's how we could support our "work in progress" (WIP) headline for the Problem and Perils.

Problem 1

Headline

The current tools Banka uses don't enable us to align our communications to the customer's actual interactions with Banka.

Supports

- Comms don't consider the type of accounts the customer has.
- Comms don't consider the usage of the accounts.
- Comms don't consider the maturity of the accounts.

Note the parts of a whole logic (MECE)

Problem 2

Headline

Banka is losing customers (especially disconnected ones) when competitors advertise heavily.

Supports

- Disconnected customers are vulnerable to advertising because they aren't aware of how Banka's services can address their unmet needs.
- Once a customer is lost, there is only a 12% chance Banka will reacquire the customer in the next 3 years.
- Attrition drives up overall marketing costs while suppressing growth because of the need to gain new customers to replace lost ones.

Note the cause and effect logic.

Perils

Headline

We need to solve the problem without adding new ones.

Supports

- We need a partner who can handle our volume.
- The solution needs to be easy to manage and integrate seamlessly with other systems.
- The solution should pay for itself in two years or less.

Note the rank order logic.

Supporting the Path

Once you've addressed the problem and perils and then supplied a promise to resolve them, it's time to move to P7— the path (how)—that must be taken to resolve the problem. Note that while this is just one stop on the road of Ps, in reality it needs to be thoroughly but simply supported. When I teach this in workshops, I always allude to Candy Land, one of those children's board games that is a rite of passage. Many times, it's the first "adventure" game that a child plays. And while there are both shortcuts and obstacles along the way to "home sweet home," the path is clear enough for a third grader to grasp.

To get to "home sweet home," you need to go past:

- ► Candy Hearts
- ► Peppermint Stick Forest
- ► Gingerbread Plum Tree
- ► Gumdrop Mountains
- ► Crooked Old Peanut Brittle House
- ► Lollipop Woods
- ► Ice Cream Floats, and
- ► Molasses Swamp.

Those are the turn-by-turn directions on the map of Candy Land that get you from here to there.

So what is *your* Candy Land path? What are the high level turn-by-turn directions you are proposing to help your Hero seize the treasure? This could be any of the three logic types (cause and effect, ranking order, parts of whole).

This is how Hank might build the Path.

Path

Headline

Banka can increase overall accounts by implementing a new intelligent onboarding program that guides customers through 3 milestones that drive expanded engagement with Banka and stickier customers.

Supports

- When a new customer enrolls at a branch (vs. being digitally acquired), the customer account will be flagged in the system for the onboarding program.
- The customer will enter the onboarding sequence designed to increase connectedness to customers
- The first milestone will be to persuade the customer to sign up for paperless communications - this allows Banka to communicate w/ the customer more meaningfully, more often, and at a lower cost than paper communications
- Once the customer registers for digital communications, they will have a completely personalized concierge-style portal and mobile app where they do their banking online.
- They'll receive various incentives to shift their primary checking account to Banka, and use Banka as their primary bill paying bank.
- Subsequent offers will be made to the customer triggered by their specific interactions with the bank designed to increase utilization (for example, credit card offers, mortgage loans, lines of credit, etc.)

Note the cause-and-effect logic, though this could be any of the 3 types of logic.

Bringing It Home

Now that the Path is clear, it's time to bring it home with proofs, a big stack of benefits (perks), and then the call to action with risk reversals (price, provocation, and protections).

Here's how that would look.

Proof

Headline

A data analysis of Banka's current customers reveals that sticky customers are the ones who have already achieved the three target milestones.

Supports

- When customers receive online communications and have their primary checking account with Banka, they are more inclined to bolt on other services to their primary account. The personal checking account serves as the hub and gateway to expanded products.
- Connected customers are 42% more likely to have a savings account with Banka
- They are 149% more likely to have a credit card account with Banka
- And they are 232% more likely to have a mortgage loan through Banka.

Note the rank order logic.

Perks

Headline

Implementing intelligent trigger-based onboarding not only saves customers from leaving for competitors, it grows business overall.

Supports

- Customers with multiple accounts stay with Banka for 10 years or more.
- Reducing churn drastically reduces re-acquisition marketing costs.
- The data tells us that increasing customers who achieve the 3 milestones by just 5% (a conservative estimate) would result in $160mm increased revenue per year.

Note the cause-and-effect logic.

Price

Headline

Diletat will cost $6.2 million to implement in year 1, and then $800k each year after.

The support would have high-level terms.

Provocation

Headline

If Banka signs an LOI before the end of the year, Diletat will run a pilot in Sacramento for Banka at cost, but if it takes longer than that they won't be able to deliver on that offer because of other commitments.

Supports

- This will allow Banka to better understand the mechanics and internal resources needed to implement the system on a wider basis.
- It will enable Banka to develop SOPs for trigger-based onboarding, and experiment with various customer messages and incentives in a tightly defined environment.
- It will allow Banka to benchmark performance of the onboarding program against a control (the other regions outside Sacramento)

Note the parts/whole logic.

Protections

Headline

Diletat will write into the LOI that if the Sacramento pilot doesn't increase customers who cross the 3 milestones by 5% in just 3 months, they will allow Banka to terminate the LOI.

Supports

- This gives Banka an exit strategy if things don't go as planned
- The tight performance window means Banka's resources would be impacted for a minimal amount of time.
- If the program isn't successful, Banka won't incur any additional costs to migrate back to Commodo. Diletat would do it at their own cost.

Note the ranking order (of importance).

Here's how to think about your storyboard and where you'll want to consider adding supports that follow Minto's pyramid principle.

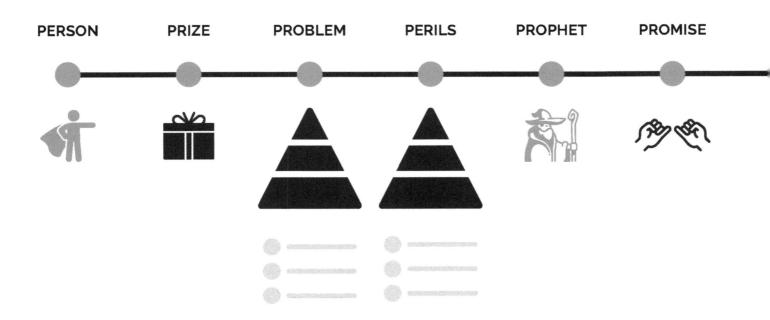

PERSON   PRIZE   PROBLEM   PERILS   PROPHET   PROMISE

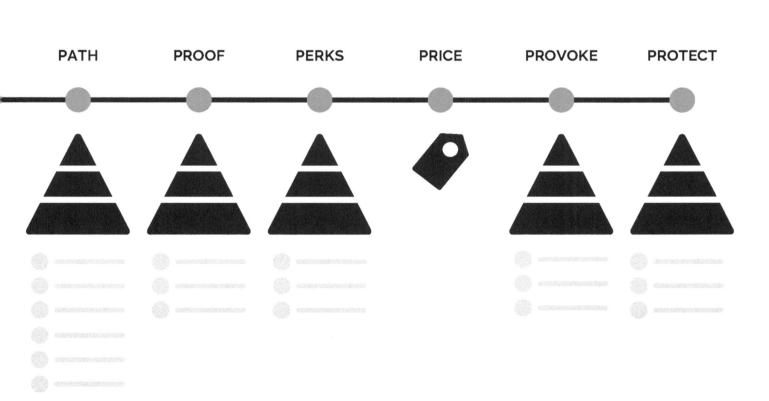

PATH   PROOF   PERKS   PRICE   PROVOKE   PROTECT

Rough Illustrations to Expand Thinking

PERSON	PRIZE	PROBLEM	PERILS	PROPHET	PROMISE
Dubious Denise	We need customers to enroll for new products.	Our current tools don't enable personalization, and we're losing customers.	We need a solution that's easy to deploy and delivers an ROI.	Hank has the answer (he's a data expert).	We need a new onboarding experience (and the tech to drive it).
		We don't account for customers current type of account(s).	Can we find a vendor who can handle our volume?		
		Don't consider usage of accounts.	What if the system doesn't integrate with other tech we have?		
		We don't account for how long we've had the customer.	The system has to be cost positive in 2 years.		

You'll find as you do this that you may spontaneously create pictures in your mind's eye as the logic clicks into place. When this happens, grab a sticky pad and capture those pictures so you can use them when you start visually designing your pages. Try to create a very simplistic doodle for each piece of your horizontal story. You can add them above your horizontal storyboard like this.

PATH	PROOF	PERKS	PRICE	PROVOKE	PROTECT
Implement Diletat, and guide new customers through 3 milestones for better retention.	Current customers that have crossed these milestones also use a wider range of products.	The new system will reduce churn and increase revenue. $$$	Diletat will cost $6.2M to implement, and then $800k/year	They're willing to run a pilot in Sacramento at cost if we sign an LOI by EOY.	If the pilot doesn't work, we can terminate the LOI.
1. New customers will get flagged for new onboarding program.	Engaged customers are 42% more likely to have a savings account.	Customers with more accounts stay 10 years or longer.		Pilot will allow us to baby-step our way in.	If pilot goes poorly, we can get out of the deal.
2. Customer will be encouraged to enroll in paperless communications.	...and 149% more likely to have a credit card.	Reducing churn will reduce marketing expense.		Will allow us to develop SOP's and design contained experiments.	Tight performance window minimizes resource impact.
3. Customer will gain access to personalized portal.	...and 232% more likely to have a mortgage with Banka.	We project $160mm increase in revenue per year.		Will enable us to benchmark Sacramento against other regions.	If pilot is unsuccessful, Diletat will revert back to current state at no cost.

Remember, don't worry about the quality of your doodles here. They are just for you to get a mental picture of each stage of your story and to help you commit your story to memory. The side benefit, which you've already seen in chapter 4 and will see again in chapter 9, is that doodling has the power to expand your thinking and understanding of just about anything.

Stories Tame Confusion

Stories allow you to take the most complex ideas and to make them understandable. Read your headline stickies. Do they make sense and carry you forward?

One of the central questions of *Inception* is whether the entire action of the movie is a dream or not. How would we know? In the movie, Cobb uses a spinning top as his "feedback" mechanism for reality. If the top stops spinning, he's in a waking state. If it doesn't, he's still in a dream. At the end of the movie, the director plays a little trick on us by not fully closing the feedback loop. The top wobbles, but the screen cuts to black before it stops spinning. We're left wondering. We can't tell which is the real world and which is Cobb's fabrication. It sticks.

By casting your Hero in a *presentation* story, they can simulate a success scenario, and that's what helps them make the decision to move forward. They can take action because they have already "practiced" the journey, anticipated obstacles, formulated solutions, and tasted victory. Your presentation is the carefully crafted simulation that enables them to do that. But it lets you do it too.

Storyboarding (or sticky-boarding in this case) will make you an expert in your material because it will simplify—in a good way—your understanding of your content. As you work through constructing the journey, all of that knowledge you gather will stick. You'll be able to give the presentation even without the slides—which could well save your bacon if you have a tech glitch or serendipitously find yourself on the elevator with your CEO.

You've got your pitch now. The next step is to shape it into pre-slides. In the next chapter, you'll take your story and build the full outline of your presentation.

Key Takeaways & Homework

▶ Stories change and shape people's minds.

▶ Create a storyboard built for persuasion using the 12 Ps.

▶ Add a sticky note headline for each P.

▶ Next, add the vertical legs of your story.

▶ Finally, create a little doodle for each horizontal P. It doesn't matter if you use it; it matters what it will do to your brain.

▶ Now, read the story. Does it make sense?

Chapter 6
Filling in Your Outline

Create a presentation outline outside of your slideware.

There's a hilarious skit from *Saturday Night Live* called "The Californians" (look it up on YouTube; it's pretty funny). It depicts a soap opera based in Los Angeles, where every conversation is peppered with traffic references.

> *Just take Manzanita down to Olympic . . .*
> *Make a right over by the Von's Pavilions . . .*
> *Take that all the way down to Robertson . . .*
> *Make a right and keep going until you see the 10.*[14]

I moved to Los Angeles in the early 2000s, and I remember finally getting how funny the skit was. In the sprawl of LA, if you have to get into your car for any reason whatsoever, you will inevitably have a conversation about what route to take to your destination. I use Waze every time I get into my car. Not because I don't know how to get to my destination, but to figure out the best route given the traffic.

---

[14] "Every Californians Ever (Part 1 of 2)." YouTube, uploaded by *Saturday Night Live,* 18 Oct. 2019, https://youtu.be/dCer2e0t8r8.

Your Deck Outline Is Like a GPS

If you're like most people, after you finish sticky-boarding, you get a powerful urge to fire up your slideware and get to banging out those slides. But hang on for just a little bit longer. There's one more step you need to take, and that's **outlining your presentation**. This should go quickly if you've got all your sticky notes organized. You've got the big ideas and your draft headlines, but what else will you say on the slide?

To help your Hero find the prize, you need to provide the right level of detail. Remember, we're trying to persuade your Hero to cross the threshold, so you need to supply a route with enough detail that they actually want to get in the car and go. The best way to do that is to outline your slides. This is the stage where you'll flex your copywriting muscles.

What Tools Should You Use to Outline?

Some of you will want to do your outlining directly in your slideware, but I urge you to resist. It's just too much of a temptation to fiddle with the design elements on your slides. That's a time-chewing rabbit hole, and at this point your time is better spent getting the "copy" of your presentation hashed out. So instead, I'm going to suggest you do what authors do and outline your storyline in a separate document. Tools are constantly changing, so while I'll point to a few tools I use personally, a simple Google search will surface others that effectively do the same thing. Here are a few to consider, and why.

My absolute favorite outlining tool is a free online tool called Workflowy (workflowy. com). At its core, it's really just a list tool, but its advantages over other tools are that your outline can be infinite. It allows you to collapse sections so you can look at your outline at a bird's-eye view with just your headlines, or expand sections and see all the details. It also lets you share your outline so others can see it and even contribute to it. It's an example of the elegance of simplicity. The only thing you can really do in Workflowy is type text in an outline form.

Another great tool is Google Docs. Google Docs is free, and I prefer it to other word processing programs because of one major advantage. Since Google Docs is cloud based, it means never "losing" my work, and it will save your revisions to infinity. So for those folks who have a hard time *"killing their darlings"* as Stephen King would say, this is the tool for you. In fact, I wrote this entire book in Google Docs. I was able to name each version I wrote at the end of my writing day, so if I ever needed to look back to a version in time, I could just go back into the virtual time capsule of the document and pull it up. Adios multiple files and version control nightmares!

Transferring Your Sticky Notes to Your Outline

Once you have chosen your outlining tool, **create a heading for each of the Ps that will be in your slide deck.**

TIP

P1 (the Person/Hero) doesn't need to be specified, so instead of having a slide for P1, we'll just add a placeholder for the Title page. The same goes for P5, though you may choose to include it to build authority.

If you're using something like Google Docs or Word, make these headings H1s, and be sure to write each heading as a complete sentence. It should look something like this. (Note, I'll continue to use the Banka example for this).

Example outline:

- Title Page
- Person
  - *Marketing VP responsible for new product promotion and customer acquisition and retention*
- Prize
  - Personalized communications are the key to improved uptake on new products.
- Problem
  - Commodo has limitations that hinder our ability to respond to customers' true needs.
  - Tone deaf communications create opportunity for our competitors to poach our customers when they advertise heavily.
- Perils (anticipate reasons for non-action)
  - We need a better solution — one that can handle our volume, integrate with existing systems, and is easy to use. (Perils)
- Prophet
  - *Our data analysis points to a solution.*
- Promise
  - Banka could grow new product uptake by implementing a more personalized onboarding experience.
- Path
  - If we guide our new customers to achieve 3 milestones in their first year with us, they are more likely to accept additional service offers.
- **Proof**
  - **Banka's customers that achieved these milestones are 82% more profitable than all other Banka customers.**
    #data, #graphic
- Perks
  - These MVCs (most valuable customers) are less likely to accept competitor offers, and stay with Banka longest.
- Price
  - An initial investment in of $6.2 million in Diletat could return $16MM+ per year for the next 3 years.
- Provocation
  - Diletat will conduct a pilot in Sacramento at cost if we sign an enterprise LOI by end of year.
- Protections
  - If new product uptake doesn't improve by 5%+ in the first 3 months of the pilot, we can cancel the LOI and Diletat will migrate Sacramento back to Commodo at their cost.

I want you to notice something here. First, because you wrote full sentences, you could literally read this as a story from top to bottom. **Your outline has become your elevator speech.** If you can commit your story to memory (and it will be easy to do in this format), you will have the equivalent of a magic wand in spreading your story. This brief outline is so powerful, I have a client who won't even look at a deck unless she sees the outline on a single page first. She says it's reclaimed 70 percent of the time she previously spent reviewing her team's PowerPoint drafts because she can spot gaps or flaws in the logic immediately.

The second thing to notice is that the story isn't about the proposed new software (Diletat) directly. Instead, the story is about solving the problem of delivering increased adoption of new products. Diletat is merely the bridge to that solution.

Confusing the bridge for the destination is one of the biggest mistakes that presentation authors (and sales and marketing professionals in general) make. Why? Because your mind plays tricks on you. Your wealth of knowledge and deliberation has led you to a conclusion—that Diletat software will provide the solution to the problem. So you naturally try to convince your Hero that Diletat is the answer. But by doing that, you deprive your Hero of the journey, and thus you deprive them from coming to an independent belief in the answer.

Always focus on the outcome your Hero seeks, not the bridge to get there. That's the power of the Ps—it focuses you on the Person (the Hero) and their Prize and flows from there.

Focus on the outcome your Hero seeks, **not the bridge to get there.**

OK, now that you have the high-level spine of your presentation loaded into your outlining software, it's time to add in your subheads and the support points that you developed in your vertical storyline. Try to stay in outline mode if you can. Though you'll find places where you need to do additional research, or want to insert an illustration or chart, just make a note of them now. Focus on getting your outline as complete as you can.

TIP

Establish a structure that simple and concise. Use H1s, H2s and so on to build out a table of contents.

Here's what the start of your outline could look like after a first draft.

Example outline:

- Title Page
- Person
  - *Marketing VP responsible for new product promotion and customer acquisition and retention*
- Prize
  - Personalized communications are the key to improved uptake on new products.
    - [illustration of customer and needs]
- Problem & Pain
  - Commodo has limitations that hinder our ability to respond to customers' true needs.
    - Currently, the way we engage with customers isn't driven by their real interactions with us.
      - We're not communicating based on the type of accounts the customer has.
      - We're not communicating based on their usage of their accounts.
      - We're not taking into consideration how long the customer has been with us.
  - Tone deaf communications create opportunity for our competitors to poach our customers when they advertise heavily.
    - Disconnected customers -- who have been with us for shorter periods of time and use their accounts minimally - are particularly vulnerable to churn.
      - Disconnected customers are vulnerable to our competitors advertising because those customers aren't' aware of how Banka can solve their unmet needs.
      - Once a customer is lost there is only a 12% chance Banka will reacquire the customer in the next 3 years.
      - Attrition drives up overall marketing costs while suppressing growth due to the need to acquire new customers to replace lost ones.
- Perils (anticipate reasons for non-action)
  - We need a better solution — one that can handle our volume, integrate with existing systems, and is easy to use. (Perils)
- Prophet
  - *Our data analysis points to a solution.*
- Promise
  - Banka could grow new product uptake by implementing a more personalized onboarding experience.
    - [illustration of 3 milestones]
- Path
  - If we guide our new customers to achieve 3 milestones in their first year with us, they are more likely to accept additional service offers.
    - By implementing a new intelligent automation system we can deploy an onboarding program that guides customers through 3 milestones that result in expanded engagement with Banka and stickier customers.
      - When a new customer is enrolled at a branch (not digitally acquired), the customer account will be flagged in the system for the onboarding program.
      - The customer will enter the onboarding sequence designed to increase

147

You already know that each P needs its own slide, but you also need to be mindful that **each slide should only express a single idea.** So sometimes, you'll need a separate slide to further illustrate a particular proof point. For example, P8 (proof) could actually be four separate slides in the presentation. The first slide would summarize the idea, and the subsequent three slides would demonstrate the proof. If you are already fairly certain that you'll want to break them out as separate slides, make a note in your outline. If you're not sure, just leave your outline as is— you'll be able to determine this later in your slideware.

P8: MVCs (most valuable customers) are less likely to accept competitor offers and stay with Banka longest.

- Implementing more intelligent trigger-based onboarding not only saves customers from leaving for competitors, it grows business.
  - P8.1 Customers with multiple accounts tend to stay with Banka for 10 years or more.
  - P8.2 Reducing churn drastically reduces re-acquisition marketing costs.
  - P8.3 The data tells us that increasing customers who achieve the 3 milestones by just 5% (a conservative estimate) would result in $160mm increased revenue per year.

Now look at your outline. How does it read? Before we head into our slide software, give some attention to the *copy*. **Make your sentences as strong as possible.**

The Power of Yada Yada

The point of writing an outline is for you to capture your thinking in a way that is clear and concise. So before you transfer your outline into your slideware, pay careful attention to words you're using to communicate your message. **Your words need to be clear, direct, and jargon-free to have the highest impact.**

If you're working on something complex, this is much harder said than done. Actually, it would be better to say harder written than done. Something weird happens when we communicate through our fingers on a keyboard—we often stop speaking plain English! Sometimes the best medicine for achieving clarity is talking it out.

Recently I was working with a strategic director on a presentation that she would take to her board of directors. Her task was to make recommendations concerning partnering with a Brazilian company in order to better penetrate the Brazil market and grow market share. The answer was not straightforward. There were so many nuances and unknowns that even teasing out the various scenarios that would make moving forward with the partnership advantageous felt like a fifty-pound hairball. She kept showing me charts, data, and skipping from one scenario to the next. There was so much information that I felt paralyzed. I couldn't follow.

Here's the thing. A lot of times, if you don't really push for clarity, your audience will feel the same. They'll have one of two conversations in their heads.

1. *"I don't get it. This person obviously gets it. I feel stupid. I'm not sure which recommendation to endorse."*

2. *"This person doesn't get it. They're all over the place. I need to find someone who can give me the information I need to make a confident decision on how to move forward."*

Neither of these thought-bubble conversations is good for you or the project. **Painfully clear communication is your secret shield against those thought-bubble conversations.** So, if you find that you're wrapping yourself around the axle, step away from your keyboard and turn to your voice. **Find someone who knows nothing about your particular topic and explain it to them.** That in itself will force you to speak clearly. And the benefit of working with someone else is that they can ask you questions if they're still not clear. Ask them to explain back to you what you said—not repeat what you said, but explain it back to you in their own words. I guarantee they will simplify what you said even better than you did.

One practice I use when I'm working with clients is to turn on my voice recorder and ask them to talk to me like I'm a third grader. I also repeat back to them what I heard to make sure it's what they meant to communicate. You'd be surprised how often that *retelling* is what makes its way onto the page.

If you don't have someone you can workshop your words with, I recommend using a recording service to capture your thoughts. At the time of this writing, services like Temi.com and Otter.ai are wonderfully easy to use. You just open their app on your smartphone or on your laptop and start talking. They transcribe what you say as you speak. The transcriptions aren't perfect, but that's not the point. The point is to see what you said because many times there's gold there. When I'm working with clients, I call it the power of yada yada (yes, I'm a massive *Seinfeld* fan).

Circle Back to Collect All the Remaining Detail

Now that you've got a good outline, it's time to go get all of that extra stuff that will add authority and color to your presentation. Gather all of your support material and create a "container" for it. Perhaps you ventured a hypothesis that needs to be supported by science, data, or a customer story. You may need to validate the steps in a workflow you referenced, or a good authoritative quote might be in order. Use whatever works for you. Just make sure it's something that can hold links and graphics.

Outlines Clarify Your Thinking and Give Your Presentation Backbone

I know outlines are old-school. But **outlines produce clear presentations while also making the actual production of your slides go faster**. If you've done your sticky note "dump and clump," turned that into your 12P Persuasion Journey, and then flowed that story into your outline, you have a rock-solid presentation in the making.

I remember when I was talking to a colleague at a multinational company. She was complaining about the presentations her team made, and I started telling her a bit about how I came up with a process that leveraged the Hero's Journey; I never go anywhere without a pack of sticky notes; I outline my slides to put them into a persuasive storytelling format, etc. I thought maybe she could take some small bit of that advice and pass it on. What surprised me is that she said she had an upcoming off-site with her team and asked if I could teach them my process. The problem: the off-site was just two weeks away!

As a consultant, of course I said yes, but I had never previously formalized my process. Now I was faced with doing an all-day workshop on presentation development, but I didn't really have a deck ready to go. Well, long story short, I used the process I'm teaching you now. I spent about ten days sticky-boarding in bursts, thinking, doing some supplemental research to support my ideas, and developing the outline. Then I developed the actual slide presentation, graphics and all, in the last two to three days.

The process works. And according to my colleague, it was the best workshop she had ever been part of in her entire career. So get to work on your outline, and stay out of your slideware as long as you possibly can. **The power of thinking outside of the slide is that it gives you more control and objectivity about your story decisions.**

Once you create something in PowerPoint, it's kind of like helping yourself to a huge serving of French fries that cover half of your plate at the buffet line before you've seen the cheesy scalloped potatoes down the line. Instead of grabbing a clean plate, you just keep piling on the potatoes. The moral of the story is, you don't want your slidework to become too precious too early in the process.

Key Takeaways & Homework

▶ Resist opening up your slideware for as long as possible.

▶ Pick the "write" tool for your outline. I prefer a combination of WorkFlowy and Google Docs.

▶ Transfer your horizontal story into your outline and use full sentences as your H1s.

▶ Transfer your vertical story supports, paying special attention to points that need their own slide.

▶ Once your outline is set, read through your outline to see if it's clear. If you're having trouble articulating a point, embrace the power of yada yada and talk it out.

▶ Finally, go back and gather all the supplemental research and support material you need and note it in your outline.

Chapter 7
Be Succinct

Why less is more, why less takes more time, and why taking your time up front will reduce total time to action in the long run.

George Orwell, a titan of the written word, penned rules for writing that every author—and especially slide authors—would be wise to post prominently wherever they build their slides:

> *Never use a long word where a short one will do. If it is possible to cut a word out, always cut it out. Never use the passive voice where you can use the active. Never use a foreign phrase, a scientific word, or a jargon word if you can think of an everyday English equivalent.*

These rules are part of Orwell's *Politics and the English Language*,[15] which he wrote expressly because he was concerned that vague writing would be used as a tool for political manipulation. He wrote it because he understood the power of language and its role in shaping how we think. And it's still true today that some political speech and writing have

a tendency to use big or vague words, jargon, acronyms, double entendres, and overused metaphors to wittingly or unwittingly intimidate, misdirect, or sometimes intentionally bore you into a catatonic stupor.

Clear and direct language is like magic. It gives your reader or audience direct access to what you really mean. Clear and direct language means your audience won't misunderstand or misinterpret your message. I could say that *it mitigates your probability of obfuscating your thesis…* but it would be better to simply say *it lowers the chances of you muddying your message.*

But there are more practical reasons to be clear and direct—because by doing so you're more likely to get what you're after in the first place and look incredibly smart while doing it.

[15] Orwell, George. *Politics and the English Language*. Penguin Classics, 2013.

Cluttered Slides Hinder Decision-Making

By saying that you must be clear and direct with your language, I don't mean be simplistic. I mean *communicate the essential* by being uncluttered. **Clarity is not possible with clutter.** Being clear and direct creates the conditions—a mental white space in your audience or reader's mind—that gives them the room to begin the inner mind journey that ultimately enables them to make their decision freely. Without clarity, your audience can't make a decision that is grounded in belief. Clutter creates the wrong sort of emotions—emotions that get in the way.

There's real science to support this. A 2011 study by the Princeton University Neuroscience Institute[16] found that **visual clutter actually affects your brain's ability to focus and make decisions.** You know that spinning ball that appears on your computer when you have too many programs open? Your brain can enter a sort of "spinning ball" state too. It happens when there are too many things "in view" that create excessive competition for processing power. **Visual clutter literally depletes your energy.** Ask people how they feel when surrounded by clutter and you'll hear words like *suffocating, anxiety,* and *irritated*.

---

[16] https://www.ncbi.nlm.nih.gov/pmc/articles/PMC3072218/

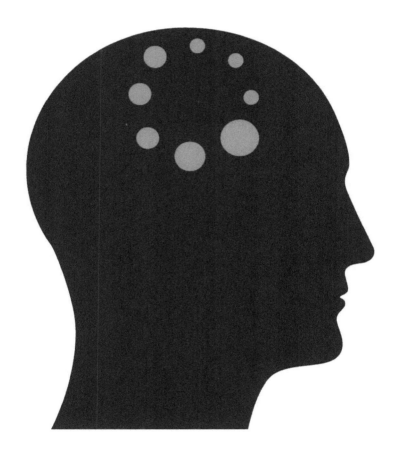

Here's the bumper sticker: **It's harder for your Hero to follow what you're saying when you say too much**. You provide too many mental off-ramps when you clutter your presentation with insider jargon, superfluous technical terms, and complicated charts and data sets. Stuffing your presentation with that garbage is a cop-out. If you insist on putting that stuff in your presentation, you better realize who you're really doing that for, and that's you! You're doing it so you look smart and can prove that you've "done the work." The problem is that it isn't helpful. **Your job as the mentor is to deliver the wisdom, not the data set.**

Herbert Simon, a noted American economist and cognitive psychologist who focused on decision-making within organizations, said it best: **"A wealth of information creates a poverty of attention."**[17] In other words, you need to keep your conversation tight, and that means keeping it succinct. If you're not lean and mean with your message—if you clutter your pages with too much stuff—you will appear confused and not only lose your audience's attention, but possibly lose their respect. Harness your inner Marie Kondo. Get to the point!

---

[17] Herbert A. Simon 1916–2001. American economist, political scientist, and computer scientist. https://www.oxfordreference.com/

Get to the Point

A clear and direct presentation demonstrates that you grasp the executive mind. Here's how to do it in three steps.

1. First, follow the general principles set out by Orwell and **use short words that are understandable by everyone**. I know that every industry has its acronyms and jargon, but no one is obligating you to use them everywhere. Consider that if you put together a truly great deck, it may find an audience beyond the people you are presenting to directly. And write in full sentences as your default. Yes, there will be places where a list of bullets is appropriate, but your deck should not be pages and pages of bullets. The headlines of your pages should be the takeaway of the entire slide. Are they making a point?

TIP

Go through your outline and read your H1s and H2s again. Are they clear, concise and jargon-free.

2. Second, **be ruthless with your editing**. Now's the time to go sentence by sentence over what you have in your outline and clean up your words. If you're using Google Docs or another outlining program that allows you to highlight your text, consider using two highlight colors. Take a bright highlighter (I use yellow) to all the essential points that support your argument. Then take a dark highlighter (I use orange) to any points that don't connect to your big idea. How does your outline look now?

    If you can read through your yellow highlights and get the full meaning of your message, bravo! Get rid of everything else. If you have a lot of orange in your outline, take the points that don't connect and find a way to connect them or get rid of them and replace them with support points that do. Chances are pretty good that your outline has more content than you really need to support your argument, so prune it now before it becomes too precious.

3. Finally, get feedback. Engage an expert or a colleague to read your edited outline and see if it makes sense. I'd also recommend you ask someone who knows nothing about the topic to review your outline as well, but give them the ground rules first. Explain your process. Tell them you're looking for feedback on the strength and quality of your argument, hypothesis, or recommendation (or whatever is appropriate). Ask them to comment on the quality of your headlines and subheadlines, as well as the logic and completeness of your supporting points where you have them. Ask them to point out places where you might have flaws in your reasoning, or things feel out of place, or where they'd like data or evidence to support your claim. Ask them for potential areas to cut.

If Google Can Do It, So Can You

I know the anxiety is probably setting in about now. You've got an incredibly complex story to tell, and you don't want to appear obtuse.

I'll remind you that most of the things that influence your behavior today are things that were both short and memorable. Moses brought down only 10 Commandments. Lincoln's Gettysburg Address was a mere eight hundred and ninety-one words. In Buddhism, the path to enlightenment is an eightfold path—just eight practices to reach enlightenment?! It doesn't sound all that complicated when you put it that way. But it sure inspires action.

But how about in decks, you say? Well, go take a look at how Eric Schmidt (former CEO and chairperson of Google) boiled his three hundred and twenty-page book *How Google Works* down to a fifty-four-page slide deck with only nine hundred and sixty words, not counting the title page![18]

▶ The title is three words: "How Google Works."

▶ Page one has twenty words: "When Jonathan and Eric arrived at Google, we thought we knew all there was to know about running successful businesses." (Notice the Person and the Prize).

---

[18] https://www.slideshare.net/ericschmidt/how-google-works-final-1

► Page two has seventeen words: "But we quickly learned that almost everything we thought we knew about managing businesses was dead wrong." (Notice the problem).

► And so on.

Seems like a children's book, doesn't it? In my workshops, I use children's books as powerful examples of how to get an emotional and visual message across. Children's books have a real economy about them. Our parents read us these stories, and they supply life lessons so we will grow up to be responsible adults that have good judgment. The best stories are so wise and simple that they end up forming the basis of how we interpret life.

Message Economy Shows Your Understanding of the Problem.

The beauty of spending time crunching down your story into a tight message is that you will massively enhance the comprehension and memory of your message. That's what increases the chance of your message spreading. It's that *"thing that sticks"* that Cobb talks about at the beginning of *Inception*.

Don't believe me? There's a reason aphorisms, proverbs, memes, and clichés stick around. It's because they pack a lot of meaning into just a few words (or images). I probably could have summed up this entire chapter with this one Dr. Seuss quote: ***"So the writer who breeds more words than he needs is making a chore for the reader who reads."***

"It has often been said
there's so much to be read,
you never can cram
all those words in your head.

So the writer who breeds
more words than he needs
is making a chore
for the reader who reads.

That's why my belief is
the briefer the brief is,
the greater the sigh
of the reader's relief is.

And that's why your books
have such power and strength.
You publish with shorth!
(Shorth is better than length.)"

~ Dr. Seuss

---

19 Seuss, Dr. (2021). A quote by Dr. Seuss. Goodreads. https://www.goodreads.com/quotes/291465-it-has-often-been-said-there-s-so-much-to-be

Let me put it this way. When it comes to authoring a presentation, whether it will be given from a stage, across a boardroom conference table, or sent off via email . . . it's **better to pierce the imagination with an arrow than pound it with a hammer**. You need a small, sharp point to plant the idea that will take root in your Hero's mind and get them to take the journey with you. If you fill their mind up with too many facts, words, or ideas, it will force them to waste precious cognitive energy sorting and categorizing all those facts versus letting the idea take flight.

And there's another benefit as well. You will make yourself smarter in the process. **You will understand the problem better as you whittle it down to its essence.** Albert Einstein said, *"If you can't explain it simply, you don't understand it well enough"* and put his money where his mouth was when he summed up his theory of special relativity with the simple equation $E=mc^2$. With a succinct presentation, sans the clutter, you'll be able to maintain your Hero's attention, and the elegant simplicity of your reasoning will inspire confidence.

Time Invested Now is Time Gained Later

Authors know that the revising and editing process is the most painful part of the writing process. In fact, if there's ever a time where you will stand back and ask yourself, *"WTF was I thinking?"* this is it. We'll address this in detail in chapters 10 and 11, but just know that you will vastly reduce the WTF factor if you take time to edit your ideas now. You'll gain distance from it. You'll start reading it through your Hero's eyes and see where you have been overly complex in places and overly contrived in others. **The sharper you make your points now, the better.**

Simplicity Sticks

Let me tell you a story about the sticking power of things stripped to their essence. I'm a foodie, and I've had some extraordinary meals. When I worked at NBC in the days of fat expense accounts, I once had a twelve-course dinner with wine pairings at a restaurant in Beverly Hills called Soma (no longer there). Do I remember what I ate? Nope. But I remember the bill for three people was thousands of dollars!

I'll tell you a meal that I believe I *will* remember for the rest of my life. It was in Porto, Portugal. It was hot out. We were tired, and my partner and I spotted a few shabby tables at the steps leading up to Sé do Porto, a Romanesque cathedral dating to the twelfth century. A man was at a barbecue pit grilling fresh sardines. Across the narrow street, a woman was bringing out plates from a doorway. *Was it a house? Was there a restaurant in there?* We still don't know. We sat down at a shaded table covered with a plastic tablecloth, ordered, and a few minutes later were presented with our meal—still sizzling charred whole sardines, a boiled potato, and a few leaves of lightly dressed lettuce on the side. Oh, and a cup of cold beer. It was divine. Three simple ingredients, but man, it was memorable.

The moral of the story? Most of the time, less is more.

When your story is ready for rewrite, cut it to the bone. Get rid of every ounce of excess fat. This is going to hurt; revising a story down to the bare essentials is always a little like murdering children, but it must be done.

~Stephen King

Once you have a tight outline, it's time to open up your slideware to start "blocking in" your presentation. Now's when you'll think about the layout of your slides and get feedback one last time before you design in earnest. We'll start doing that in the next chapter.

Key Takeaways & Homework

▶ Less is more.

▶ A cluttered mind creates cluttered slides, and too many ideas log-jam the brain's processing power, making it hard to focus and make decisions.

▶ You need to create mental white space for your audience to have the room to feel something that they can rationalize.

▶ Get to the point. Check your slides to make sure you're using clear, direct, succinct, and jargon-free language.

▶ Simplifying a complex message will make you smarter and make you appear smarter too.

▶ Cut to the bone now to save time later.

Chapter 8
Copy-blocking Pages in Your Slideware

Apply design principles to your slides
and get feedback early.

Your Page Layout Matters

Nobody ever means to create a deck that has page after page of word wallpaper, but it happens. It happens (as I hope you've fully digested by now) when you think *into* your slideware. It also happens when you don't carefully consider how your deck will be consumed.

Lately, people use slide decks for just about everything. You rarely see an old-fashioned letter, or memo, or portrait-oriented document in the workplace anymore. Everything is in landscape now. But should it be? What does layout have to do with any of this?

Before you commit to the layout of your slides, take a minute to ask yourself how the slides will be consumed.

► As a pre-read?

► With a voiceover to what's on the slides?

► Mostly to support an oral presentation?

► Will folks get it in advance?

- ▶ Will it be viewed on a personal screen or on a projected screen?

- ▶ Will it have to stand on its own with no voiceover support at all?

- ▶ How familiar is the audience with the topic?

- ▶ Is this a conference room–style presentation, or a stage-style presentation?

- ▶ Is it for an internal or external audience?

- ▶ Is it mostly to inform and get buy-in?

- ▶ Are you looking for guidance? Or sponsorship? Or endorsement? Or evangelism?

- ▶ Or does it need to persuade and "close" a decision by the end of the presentation?

What, ultimately, do you want to have happen when you stop talking, or when they stop reading?

The answers to these questions are going to determine how dense or austere your pages will be. A fundamental question to ask yourself is, **is the presenter or the presentation itself leading?**

If the presenter's leading, the deck you're building is there to support what you're saying and hopefully provide some mnemonic (memorable) hooks to help what you're saying "stick." **If you're presenting in a live environment, whether in a room or virtually, your slides will primarily be visual reinforcements to what you're saying verbally.**

Very often it's the actual *content* within the presentation that will lead. This is the case when you send an electronic copy of your presentation to attendees in advance of a meeting as a pre-read. In this case, folks need to comprehend what you're communicating *without* the benefit of you explaining it. Later, during the actual presentation, you'll present a scaled-back version of your deck.

Get The Feel of Your Presentation as a Whole

At this stage in the process, you have a very good grasp of the story you want to tell and the outcome you intend to get. You know the basic turn-by-turn directions that your Hero must take. But have you ever sat down to actually write directions for someone and found yourself a little stumped by how best to guide the person? Sometimes, what you know intuitively is challenging to communicate to someone else. How much information will you need to supply to get your Hero from where *they* are to where *you* are?

Whether or not you realize it, even with all the work you've been doing to get your thoughts out of your head, and all the time you've spent doing a fairly detailed outline, your thoughts are still not presentation-ready. That's because explaining it to someone else is a whole other thing. Now's the time to draw up the map that someone *else* can understand, which means it's time to transition to your slideware and start copy blocking. It's time to create *your* version of *How Google Works*. If you went back and inspected that deck, what you'd notice is that there's always a combination of text and illustrations on the pages. And, while the *How Google Works* deck isn't constructed with headlines per se, you could easily infer what they might be with just a quick read.

TIP

Get a feel for the layouts that work for your subject matter by researching decks from companies like Gartner, Deloitte, and others on the internet.

Copy blocking is about getting a good mental image of the design of your presentation. Depending on your particular use case, you'll "block" your presentation differently.

What you'll do now is use a combination of your slideware, your stickies, and a Sharpie to block your pages. As you begin to build your presentation in your slideware, you'll begin the artisan part of the process. It's where you'll give your story a voice, tone, and shape.

Here are the broad steps you'll take to copy block your presentation.

1. Add headlines to your slideware and print out your pages (or transfer them to a digital paper program).

2. Draw in rough illustrations or charts.

3. Block in where your more detailed copy will go with some lorem ipsum.

4. Use the rule of thirds to guide your general layout.

5. Review the totality of your deck. Do you need transition slides? Do you need to explain a point over several pages? Is there anything you can remove?

6. Now go back into your slideware to finish blocking your presentation.

Note: if you have a great deal of discipline, you can do the entire exercise in your slideware, but it could end up taking you longer if you're not careful.

Let's review the steps in detail. **The first step is to add your headlines.** Now, if you're like most people, you're going to notice something immediately, and that's that some of your titles (or headlines) are way too long! **See how you can pare your headlines down to the most clear and essential statements.** They should still be in the form of a full sentence, and the statements should also be able to stand on their own without needing to read the headline of the previous slide.

Next, **print out your pages** or use an app that you can draw onto. I create all of my headlines in my slideware of choice and then export the entire deck as a PDF and import it into the Notability app on my iPad.

Banka is losing customers (especially disconnected ones) when competitors advertise heavily.

This is the printout of a Banka slide with a title.

For the next step, on either your physical piece of paper or your digital paper, **draw your rough illustrations or charts** into the space that you expect it to occupy on the page. The size of the illustration will depend on the use cases (i.e., self-contained, meeting, or stage).

This is the printout with my graphic drawn in, which gives me a sense of how much room I have for copy. This example would be for a standard meeting or "table presentation." The graphic is the star, but I'll add enough text to explain the graphic for anyone that will want a soft copy of the presentation. I know that in the actual presentation, I'll say more than is written on the page.

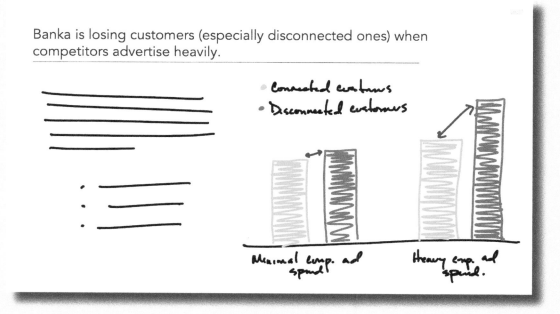

This is an example of how my slide might look if I'm sending the presentation as a pre-read to someone and won't be able to explain what they're consuming in person. Notice I've left plenty of room to add context.

Banka is losing customers (especially disconnected ones) when competitors advertise heavily.

And finally, this is what the slide might look like if I plan to present from a stage or a venue where most of the attention would be on me. (In fact, I could even remove the title altogether, but I want you to have a sense of the process of adapting a single slide to three distinct use cases.)

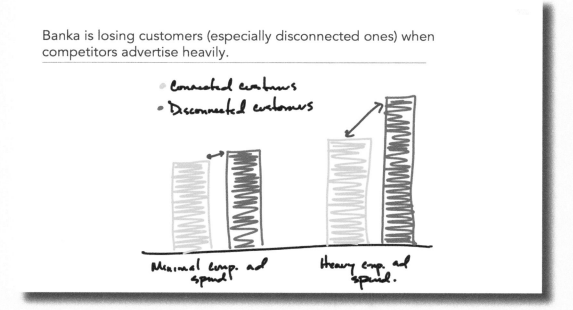

Could you do this directly in your slideware? Of course! But if you did, you'd be denying the part of your brain that has the greatest power to persuade—the creative and emotional side.

The Power of the Pen

I've already praised the power of doodling, but when you doodle with constraints, you really take your thinking mind to another level. **There's a magical connection between your brain and your hand.** In many ways, it's one of the distinguishing characteristics of humankind. You'll notice that as you *draw your pages*, and especially as you build charts with a pen, you have to simplify what's complex. **Sketches are good proofs of concept for your ideas and thinking.** If your thinking is still too complex, this is the step where it will catch up with you. If your idea is too vague, it will be hard to capture it in a simple hand-drawn illustration or chart.

But what if you don't really have a chart or relevant illustration for a page? Well, it depends. If you plan on filling the page with a lot of text, you've got a problem. We've gone through all the reasons before, but the most important one is that people will glaze over when you get to that page and will have a hard time remembering what it said. So instead of just drawing a page full of text and pushing on, force yourself to doodle something. Anything!

You can create mental concepts from word ideas too. For example, I could use a page full of text to explain the dynamic between the prework of building a slide deck, the blocking, the writing, the layout and design, making sure your thinking is sound, and even pre-warming the audience all the way to the actual presentation of the deck. But would you remember it all? Doubtful. Or I could build a very simple graphic.

Here's what that could look like in two takes.

Doodle #1: In this version, I was taking all of my information and trying to put it on a timeline that represented how much time each step takes.

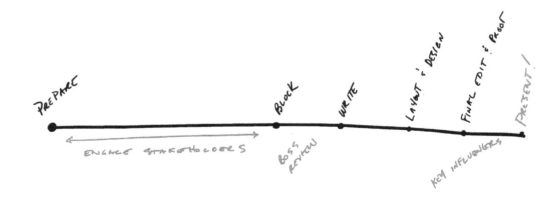

After looking at it for a minute or two, I realized that it wasn't very satisfying or memorable. So I kept thinking and came up with this version to explain how much each step really takes and who to engage when.

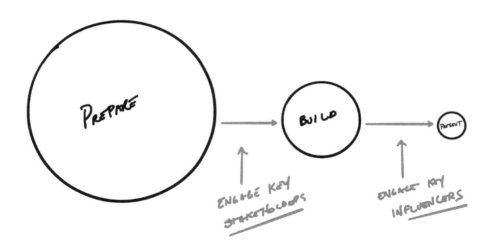

Doodle #2 is much simpler, but has a greater impact. You can see that preparation is what will take the longest in terms of time and that you should take care to engage *stakeholders* before you build. You can also see that after you've started building your slides, you'll want to engage key *influencers* as the deck takes shape in order to pre-seed buy-in leading up to the actual presentation.

As you start to visually lay out your pages, you'd also be wise to **think about the *rule of thirds***. You might have noticed that when you take photos on your smartphone, there's a subtle grid on the viewfinder that looks like a tic-tac-toe pattern. The reason for that grid is that photos that have their focal point aligned to the intersections are more pleasing and natural than photos that put the focal point dead center. The same is true for your slides. **As you draw your slides, think about arranging your information across thirds of the page** like this.

Here's the rule of thirds applied to a text-dense page.

Let the text do most of the talking.

Use this layout for a pre-read.

The core of your idea summarized in less than 10 words

Expand on your idea. Tell why it matters, and why the listeners should care. Be informative, but also be interesting. Tell the story in a way that would resonate with your audience. Don't be afraid to throw in a joke, an unexpected metaphor, or a silly pun.

Another idea, equally important

A presentation is the process of presenting a topic to an audience. It is typically a demonstration, introduction, lecture, or speech meant to inform, persuade, inspire, motivate, or to build good will or to present a new idea or product.

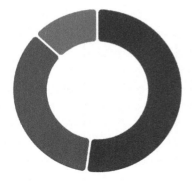

You can apply it to a table-style presentation like this.

Let the graphic do most of the talking.
Use this layout when for your 'table' presentation.

This is space for you to expand. Just start typing away. Write as much as you want (or as little, if you're channeling Hemingway).

- A little Lorem ipsum to get your creative juices flowing.
- Lorem ipsum dolor sit amet, consectetur adipiscing elit. Morbi rutrum consectetur dolor pulvinar pharetra.
- Aesthetic put a bird on it umami small batch snackwave forage beard fixie.

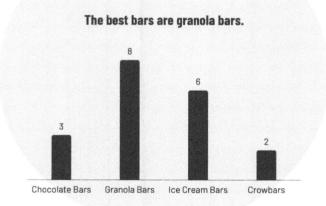

The best bars are granola bars.

Chocolate Bars	Granola Bars	Ice Cream Bars	Crowbars
3	8	6	2

Or you can apply it to stage presentations like this.

Persuasion Needs to Happen Throughout the Process

Once you've gone through all of your pages and tightened up the titles, and then blocked in where you'll tell your visual story and place your text, stand back and look at the thing as a whole. When we work on client projects, we like to print out all the pages and put them on the wall according to our horizontal and vertical storyboard to get a proper sense of the flow.

With the titles and illustrations you've drawn in, are you able to get a sense of the entire presentation? Now's a great time to invite some of your key stakeholders to take a look and validate that you're representing the story in a way that makes sense and that also drives your Big Idea.

As you cross over to the build stages of your presentation, remember that the point of your presentation is to *persuade*. And **in order to persuade, you have to make people feel something**. The more opportunities you create to make people feel something, the better. So pull in a few of your Hero's trusted advisors in the company to review your work in progress. Ask them for their feedback. Find out where they still have unanswered questions or perhaps don't agree with your logic. It's much better to address those issues now rather than in the room. The benefit of getting their feedback at this stage, when they're reacting to your titles and doodles (versus reacting to draft pages), is that they'll understand that they're looking at a work in progress. Since the cake is not fully baked, they can provide input without derailing the work you've done so far.

Most importantly, **when your stakeholders have provided input prior to you finalizing the deck, they have marked it in a way. They have skin in the game. When they see the finished product, they will believe that they have had a hand in getting it there. That's how you get buy-in.**

Block Your Pages in Your Slideware

Once you've gotten your feedback and revised your thinking appropriately, it's time to go into your slideware and block in where you will place your visuals, assuming you have some. Then transfer in your subtitles and preliminary copy. Start *refining* your copy—making it tighter and more distilled. Remember, if you will be giving this presentation with voiceover, you only need to write enough to complement your idea or visual. Your audience shouldn't read everything you plan to say.

How Good is Your Map?

The power of working a hybrid step into your deck-building process, using both your slideware and hand-drawn illustrations, is that it gives you the ability to stress test how well you are communicating what you know. **Your presentation is a bit like a treasure map. Its purpose is to guide your Hero from where they currently are, past the obstacles that could hold them back, to the outcome they desire. You are the guide.** You are their GPS. But it's not enough to know where the treasure is; **you have to tell them how to get to the treasure in a way they will understand and help them believe that the journey is worth their while**. The blocking of your presentation is what allows you to do that. It establishes the language you'll use— both visual and written—and allows you to ensure that your audience will understand what you actually mean to communicate. It's the beta test of your deck that you do before you go to full production.

Congratulations! It's time to go into production! In the next chapter, you'll start to further develop your visual language.

Key Takeaways & Homework

▶ Determine the use case of your presentation. Will it need to be freestanding (without the aid of your voiceover)? Will it supplement your spoken presentation but also be used as a shareable artifact? Or is it primarily to complement a one-way presentation from the stage?

▶ Transfer your headlines to your slideware and then copy block your pages using the rule of thirds.

▶ Harness the power of the pen for your visuals. Make them simple and intuitive.

▶ Stress test your story at this stage by getting input from stakeholders and key influencers.

▶ Once you've calibrated with stakeholders and influencers, transfer the content into your slideware.

Chapter 9

Using the Power of Visuals to Make Your Slides Memorable

How memory works, how emotions help encode memory, and **why visuals make your content sticky**.

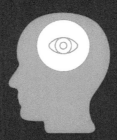

What's a Favorite Memory You Have?

Try this thought experiment. Think of your favorite vacation. Now recall a time you were excited and scared at the same time. How about a time you disappointed yourself? Take a minute and call these memories forward in your mind.

Take those memories and *imagine* yourself putting them into the box here. Don't write them down—just mentally deposit them into the box.

- **Memory 1**

- **Memory 2**

- **Memory 3**

Next to that box that you've mentally filled, jot down a quick bullet of what each memory was about.

What happened during that brief thought experiment? If you're like most people, you retrieved a combination of mental pictures or movies. Now compare that with what you wrote down. Pretty different, isn't it?

That's the thing about memory. It's largely visual. In all the times I've been doing this exercise in workshops, no one has ever told me they remembered text on a page or imagined letters that combined to make up a word. **We have to remember that text is simply code.** If you're reading this in English, it means that you learned twenty-six symbols that represent sounds—the alphabet. You have the ability to mix these symbols together to create phonological sounds (words) that represent ideas and concepts. But the words are not the same as the concepts; they're really just shorthand.

The Brain is Largely Visual

Vision is the most highly developed of all the senses. In fact, 90 percent of the information that is sent to the brain is visual. And half of the human brain is directly or indirectly devoted to processing visual information.[20] This makes sense when you think about the way we evolved and how all land animals evolved, really. One thing I've always found so fascinating is how different animals evolved to have their eyes in different places depending on what type of environment they inhabit. A crocodile, for example, has bulgy eyes that sit just above the surface of the water like twin periscopes to spot prey. Then there are animals like horses that have eyes on the sides of their heads. And an owl's enormous eyes enable it to see well at night. But did you know that an owl doesn't really have peripheral vision? Its eyes can't move—they're literally fixed into place by bone. That's why owls have to turn their heads side to side to see. Animals' ability to process visual information quickly is vitally important for both hunting and spotting predators.

Our visual sense is so acutely tuned, and our inclination to seek out visual information is so strong, that you can see why planting visuals into your presentation will give it a much higher likelihood of being remembered. **Our brains are wired to see and remember things in a way that's very different from remembering text on a page. And, when you combine**

[20] https://www.seyens.com/humans-are-visual-creatures/.

the power of visual memory with a storytelling narrative structure, you can do something even more powerful to aid memory. You can manufacture emotion. When you create a visual story, you're guiding your audience through a simulated experience that will cause them to anticipate, wonder, react, and form a point of view that will compel them to agree (or perhaps disagree) with what you're saying. And at the end of the day, that emotion is what they need to move them to a decision.

To give you a sense of how much more important your visual sense is than other senses, consider this. Neuroscientist John Medina said that **if you hear a piece of information, three days later you'll remember 10 percent of it. But if you add a picture to that information, three days later you'll remember 65 percent of it**.[21] That's a big difference! And that's because the ability to either comprehend a mental image or to manifest a mental image in your mind takes you on a journey and constructs a thing that is inherently more memorable.

---

[21] Medina, J. (2009). Brain rules. Pear Press.

Visuals Make Presentations More Persuasive

So far, you've been sketching and doodling to help you *think*. But now it's time to consider how to *communicate* with your visuals. When we think of communication, the first things that usually come to mind are words, but **for presentations, visuals rule.** It's better to plan your visuals early and subsequently write the copy you'll need to complement your visuals rather than the other way around. In fact, a University of Minnesota study concluded that **presentations with visual aids are 43 percent more persuasive than text-based presentations alone.**[22] Visuals encapsulate entire universes of meaning in a way that words on a page simply can't. **Visuals have the ability to represent concepts, ideas, connections, events in time—stories—that can be grasped as a whole.** Words, on the other hand, have to be interpreted.

How many times have you gotten trapped in one of those conversations where you debated over the meaning of a word? Here's one example. I had been working

[22] https://www.seyens.com/humans-are-visual-creatures/

for over a year with a client to develop a network of internal digital screens for communications to visitors, kind of like a closed-circuit broadcast network. We had finally selected a vendor and were working to finalize the contract when we realized that the vendor and my client had two different understandings of the word "template." The vendor was using the word "template" to describe how they would map different feeds of data to the digital screens. But my client was using "template" to describe the graphical layout and styling of the screen, much like a PowerPoint template. I vividly remember a meeting where we were talking in circles until my client finally brought up a screen on her computer and said, "This is one of our templates." Suddenly there was clarity. The moral of the story is that words don't always suffice, but seeing is believing. And **believing is what persuades your Hero to cross the threshold**.

Communication with Visuals Predates Written Language

Consider the evolution of communication. The first *written* language that we've found is Sumerian, dating to just about 3000 BC.[23] It evolved from cuneiform[24]—a shape-based written language dating as far back as 4000 BC. But the oldest cave art[25] that has been found (in Borneo) is from about forty thousand to fifty-two thousand years ago! Let that soak in for a second. **We were communicating with visual language literally tens of thousands of years before we developed a written language.**

Probably the oldest known painting, from the cave of Lubang Jeriji Saléh on the Indonesian island of Borneo, circa 40,000 BC.

Trilingual cuneiform inscription of Xerxes I at Van Fortress in Turkey, written in Old Persian; A list of gifts, Adab, 26th century BC

[23] https://en.wikipedia.org/wiki/Sumerian_language
[24] https://en.wikipedia.org/wiki/Cuneiform
[25] https://en.wikipedia.org/wiki/Prehistoric_art#/media/File:Lubang_Jeriji_Sal%C3%A9h_cave_painting_of_Bull.jpg

In Greek and Roman times, orators used the "loci method" to build memory palaces to help them recall what they wanted to say in their speeches. They took a familiar space they could imagine *visually* and attached key parts of their speech to different areas in that space.

More recently, in the Middle Ages, stained glass windows were used extensively in cathedral buildings to illustrate the stories and lessons of the Bible to a mostly illiterate population. (See the poor man's Bible from the Canterbury Cathedral.[26]) When you think about it, those stained glass window panels are a lot like our modern-day slides. The purpose of our slides should be to tell a story that helps guide our audience to quickly grasp a concept in its entirety so they can make a good decision. In order to do that, your **visuals need to convey meaning**.

[26] https://en.wikipedia.org/wiki/Poor_Man%27s_Bible#/media/File:Canterbury_Cathedral_020_Poor_Mans_Bbible_Window_01_adj.JPG

Embrace Your Role as a Designer

So how can you, as a nonartist, build visuals that will convey the meaning you need to communicate and be memorable enough to guide behavior? Well, you'll have to think like designers think. **What separates a designer from everyone else is thinking intentionally**. Designers put the use of the thing they're designing at the center of all design decisions they make, and that's what you'll need to do. You must think about how to design a visual story that enables your Hero to grasp—not read—the message that will help them decide.

One way to cultivate your designer's mind is to **think about the verb that you want your presentation to do**. For example, will it *explain* a problem or *illuminate* a solution? Will it *connect* ideas? *Instigate* action? *Guide* a decision? When you are thoughtful about your verb, it will make you see your slides in a whole new way.

Think about what you need to illustrate to bring your communication to life. Revisit your outline. You'll want to let the message drive your visualization. Depending on the message, you might use **diagrams, charts, tables, or even photographs**. But beware of dumping ready-made visuals into your slides. If the meaning isn't immediately apparent, you'll need to adapt them. Sometimes, for example, when you need to visualize an insight that was produced by data, you'll want to *emphasize the insight or takeaway over the data itself*. Though the insight may have come from looking at a chart, you may realize it would be better to transform it into a diagram, or vice versa.

Try sketching your idea quickly to capture how your mind automatically wants to organize the concept. Get all the ideas at least started, but prepare to abandon a sketch mid-thought if you need to capture the next one. It's easier to go back and finish an idea you've started and abandoned than to try to remember one that flashed across your mind but never got noted. This will take a bit of practice. Try to make a habit of attaching a few sketches to any notes that you create. The more you do it, the more you'll get in tune with the mental images and concepts that your brain is creating naturally.

Use the Right Type of Visual for the Right Purpose

As I mentioned previously, there are different types of visuals that will bring your ideas to life and make them more memorable.

▶ **Diagrams** are used to convey things like relationships, flow, order, and sequences. They could be used to represent systems, the way things are organized, or parts of a whole.

▶ **Charts,** on the other hand, are primarily about bringing data to life. They'll be used to quantify things with more accuracy than a diagram can and to show relative sizes or impacts.

▶ **Tables** are handy for categorizing things and putting information into structured compartments.

All of these—diagrams, charts, and tables—are abstract concepts. You don't see them out in the physical world, but they appear in your mind's eye all the time if you start paying attention.

An equally important type of visual is photographs. These are great for conjuring emotion in presentations. A photograph might be just the thing you need to allow your audience to build a memory in their minds, imbued with their own meaning. There's even some science around where and when you should place certain slides that will stimulate the brain and make it ready to receive an important message.[27]

As you start to sketch, don't forget about the seven questions and six slide types. Ask yourself which type of question your slide is answering and sketch a visual to suit.

1. Who
2. What
3. Where
4. How many / much
5. When
6. How
7. Why

[27] http://www.slideclub.com/

To convey a complex idea, you might need to combine some of those diagrams together. A chart, for example, will often represent how many and when at the same time. A common org chart features a combination of who, what, and where.

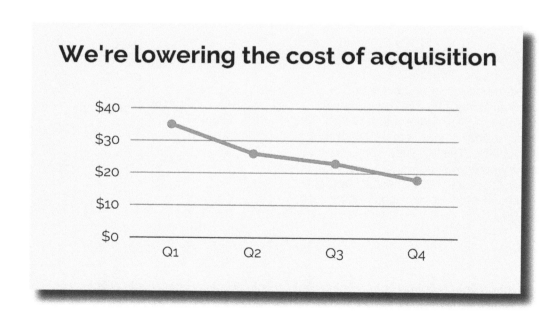

Don't overcomplicate your visual. Most charts should only convey the information that is absolutely necessary. If you're concerned about getting asked about how you arrived at your hypothesis or that you'll be asked to justify your conclusions, **put the full data set in the appendix**. This is also something you should do if you're sending your presentation as a pre-read.

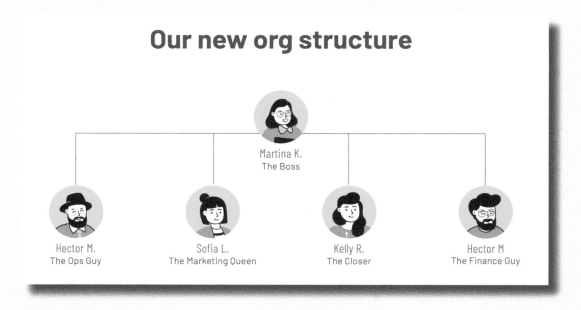

Do You Need a Graphic Artist?

In some companies, for high-stakes presentations, you will enlist a graphic designer to support your presentation project. But for most people, this is not the case. It's one reason slide templates are a dime a dozen on the internet. Folks go searching for templates so they can make their slides "look" better. I'm going to be controversial right now and tell you that **searching for the perfect template is a waste of your time**. If you are in a position to enlist the help of a designer to bring your insights and conclusions to life, fantastic! But if you aren't, that's perfectly fine too. Because either way, the ideas are going to start with you. A designer will ask you what you're trying to convey, so you're going to need to spend some time thinking

about it regardless. Instead of looking for a fancy template, you'd be wiser to spend the time doodling in a notebook or sketching rough diagrams on a sticky note without languishing over whether your doodles are good. Trying to make your point visually will stimulate your brain and help you make new connections.

Or, if you're drawing a blank or need a break, either go for a walk (Steve Jobs and others are famous for using walking to work out problems), or just open up a magazine or a children's book for inspiration. Magazine and children's book publishers spend a lot of time figuring out how to blend words, pictures, and illustrations. Two magazines I recommend for simple but potent graphics are *The New Yorker* and *Harvard Business Review*. Follow them on LinkedIn and you'll see what I mean.

Doodle-sketching your visualization will help you home in on how to make your point as simply as possible. Do what designers do and doodle several different ways of representing your point. Try to do three or four or more sketches to get to the right one. Iterate. Do it in pen so you HAVE to redo your work. The movement of drawing will open up new pathways in your brain (it's called kinesthetics).

Once you've gotten to your idea on paper, go into your slideware and create a graphic that captures what you sketched. Don't overcomplicate it. Use simple shapes and minimal colors. Less is more here because it gives your reader or audience an opportunity to fill the white space with their own thinking.

TIP

Constraints can be good. If you're not visually inclined, stick to basic shapes and lines to organize your ideas.

The Power of White Space for the Wandering Mind

When I help leaders with their slides, one thing I inevitably have to help them do is cut, cut, cut. I try to **create white space on the page and breathing room in the deck overall**. Why? Because you have to give your audience the time and space to let their minds wander. Wandering is where the magic happens. When you plant the seed of an idea with just a few words and an image that is "just enough" to get the wheels turning, you launch your audience into an internal journey—and that internal journey is essential to persuasion. Logic is all well and good, but the brain is trying to make meaning of all the input that it's getting from the senses. The sensing happens first, and then the logic or "meaning-making" kicks into gear.

Persuasion happens internally. People persuade *themselves*. So, the more you do to fire up the senses to engage your readers in a multimodal way (with a combination of reading, listening, and seeing), the more they will make "sense" of what you're communicating and arrive at the desired conclusion.

People can hold many more mental images in their minds at one time than they can hold on to a list of words, much less a list of bullet points. Your job is to tell them what they're supposed to "take away" from all of those bullet points. You want them to *envision* what you're saying. **If you can make them see something—really "get it"—then you can make them feel something**. You're giving your Hero the tinder to spark a fire that will help them decide.

The Interior Design of Your Deck

Like most people, to buy our "forever" home, we first had to sell our previous home at the highest price possible. Luckily, we had the help of a phenomenal agent. She came into our old house that was open and breezy but obviously lived-in and said, "You need a home stager. I'm going to hire someone to spruce this place up." I was a weensy bit offended. We pride ourselves on having an uncluttered and tidy home, but we soon learned that clean and tidy wasn't the issue.

When the home stager came in, she had two goals: 1) depersonalize our home, and 2) add touches that could make the buyers imagine *themselves* inhabiting our space (without us!). What was even more interesting, though, is that she could do this with stuff she already had in her truck.

Think about that for a minute. Even though our house was unique, she had stuff that she used in other styles of homes that would work in our house. Hmm, how did she do that?

Well, she had the equivalent of a "toolbox" of stuff that would always work. First, she depersonalized. When she got to work boxing many of my books, I died a little on the inside because I'm obsessed with books and think it's impossible to have too many. But she said it was too much visual clutter—too much for the eye to take in. We didn't want people marveling at all the books and not looking at the rest of the house. She also removed a lot of personal pictures. To put it plainly, we needed the equivalent of white space. Sound familiar?

The next thing she did was add little accents here and there. The idea was to create a "canvas" that represented an idea of how the buyers would want to live. Have you ever noticed how some hotel rooms are so well-designed you could imagine living your entire life there—even though they're just a big room with a bathroom? Well, that's the idea. So she artfully added arranged books and curiosities on the coffee table (but hid our army of remotes). She added pops of color with accent pillows to the couch. Fresh fruit in a bowl went on the kitchen counter. She added what looked like fresh flowers to the bathroom! Who puts fresh flowers in the bathroom? Outside, by the pool, she added a cute little table and chairs, and on the table went a wine bucket with fake ice, a bottle of wine, and two wineglasses on an artful tray. By the time she was done, we thought twice about moving at all. Was this really our space? Why didn't we think of that?

I bet you're starting to see this scene, aren't you? But I haven't even told you anything about the house other than that it has a living room, kitchen, bedroom, bathroom, and a pool. It doesn't matter! Your imagination took off. And that's what you need to do with your decks. You need the equivalent of that truck with stuff you can use just about anywhere, and here it is. Let's start filling your visual design toolbox.

Your Visual Design Toolbox

Pages with visuals help your audience remember what you're saying. You already know that. But which visuals? It helps to have a handful of go-tos, so here are a few ideas to keep in your arsenal. Copy this page and keep it handy wherever you work on your slides.

Comparisons

You're probably most familiar with comparison diagrams and charts. Anything that seeks to answer this versus that, or here versus there, is a comparison.

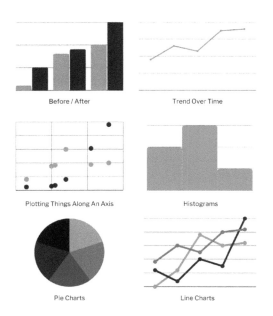

Before / After

Trend Over Time

Plotting Things Along An Axis

Histograms

Pie Charts

Line Charts

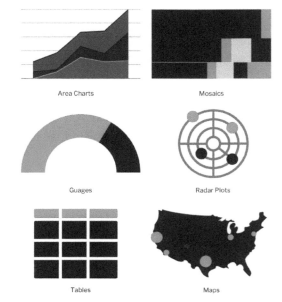

Area Charts

Mosaics

Guages

Radar Plots

Tables

Maps

Processes

Process diagrams are what you use for things that happen over time (or simultaneously). Process charts always have an element of time, sequencing, or priority.

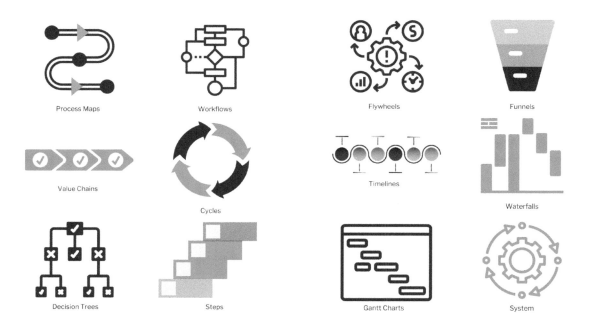

Process Maps

Workflows

Flywheels

Funnels

Value Chains

Cycles

Timelines

Waterfalls

Decision Trees

Steps

Gantt Charts

System

Structure & Systems Charts

And then there are pictograms or icons. These convey an idea more literally in a simple image. Icons differ from symbols, which have a universal meaning that is

not directly represented in the image. For example, the male and female images on bathroom doors are pictograms or icons, whereas the image that has a circle with a line through it is a universal symbol for "do not."

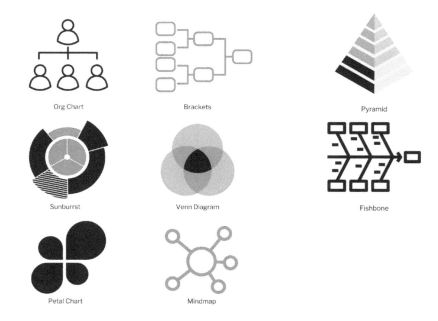

Org Chart

Brackets

Pyramid

Sunburrst

Venn Diagram

Fishbone

Petal Chart

Mindmap

Pictograms

Icons

Use this to stimulate your thinking when you're trying to figure out how to visualize something.

Layout

Now let's get macro. You have an idea of some things you can put on the page, but how should you lay out the page? In interior design–speak, which wall are you going to put the bed against, the dresser drawers, and how about that potted plant you've been hauling around for the last seven years?

Layout is all about determining in advance where you want to draw the eye and making sure you have enough room to let the eye roam. You wouldn't fill a room corner to corner with furniture, so you shouldn't do that with your slides either. Decide what the most important piece of furniture on the page needs to be. In a bedroom, it's the bed. In the living room, it's the couch. What's the most important piece of furniture on your slide? What needs to dominate?

Movement & Animation

I'm going to go ahead and say it right now. **I'm not a fan of animation in slides**. Most of the time it equates to my "too many books" problem. Animations can be distracting and can even make you look foolish if they come off as hokey. I would be perfectly fine if you skip this little section altogether. Trust me, your readers won't EVER miss an animation.

At the same time, there are exceptions to every rule. Sometimes (not many!) an animation will work so well that your audience didn't even realize it was there because it was so native to leading them through the story that it was practically invisible. Animations work best when you are doing active presenting. (In other words, they don't work for a printed piece.)

Layout

Here's an example.

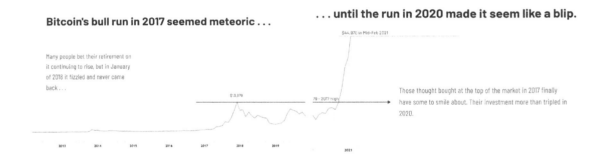

The slide animates to reveal a part of the story. This works well when you are presenting a before/after or comparison type of visual, and it works particularly well with panoramic true-life images over abstract images. You could also use abstract images if you take care to provide continuity from page to page.

Key Takeaways & Homework

▶ The brain is largely visual.

▶ Using visuals in presentations makes them 43 percent more effective.

▶ As a presentation author, you should also embrace your role as a designer.

▶ Use diagrams, charts, tables, and photographs to answer the questions of Who, What, Where, How Many, When, How, and Why. (And sketch them before you design them in your slideware.)

▶ Build up your toolbox of visual elements for comparisons, processes, systems, and structures. But keep them simple!

▶ Don't forget to leave enough white space for the imagination to have room to roam.

▶ If you must use animation, use it sparingly.

Chapter 10

Begin Building Your Slides

How to build slides without disappearing down the PowerPoint rabbit hole.

One thing that always surprises me when I coach executives is that when they have to talk about their deck's topic, they can do it really easily. In fact, all I usually do is ask the questions that will enable me to storyboard their 12 Ps, and the words flow out of them effortlessly and authoritatively.

Here's another thing I've noticed. The less I know about the topic, the clearer the executives are. That's because they can't resort to all of their industry or company acronyms and don't need to prove they are smarter than I am. My ignorance of the topic combined with their experience automatically gives them the advantage of being the experts. When I play Columbo,[28] there's no need for them to assume the role of Einstein. Then, after we talk, I ask them to send me everything I would need to build out in slides what they just told me in words. And surprise! I get the equivalent of the Old Testament instead of just getting the 10 Commandments.

When I come back a few days later and present a draft that's just a handful of pages and written in plain and direct language, accompanied by mostly austere visuals, they marvel. Wow, you really got to the meat of the message. How long did it take? The reality is they gave me the answers in their talk. I captured everything on sticky notes, and all those extra pages they gave me were just backup.

---

[28] Oh, Columbo! Columbo was a homicide detective played by Peter Falk in a TV show that aired mostly in the seventies. His schtick was to play a seeming inept ignoramus who was always asking dumb questions, but little by little got the culprit to reveal his or her motive.

PowerPoint: The Agony & Ecstasy

There's an old Hunter S. Thompson quote about the television business being a "cruel and shallow money trench…where good men die like dogs."[29] In some ways, the same could be said about PowerPoint. **PowerPoint is a cruel and gaping time suck—an inescapable rabbit hole where bullets fly, "anecdata" runs free, and good ideas die from emotional malnutrition.**

The reality is that **PowerPoint is simultaneously your greatest ally and your worst enemy**. It has the power to distract you with mindless tasks while eating the time you should use to craft a message that will stir your audience's emotions. Like it or not, for most of you, once you get into the PowerPoint zone, you will want to start tinkering with the formatting. I know from experience what it's like to think that if I can just find the perfect icon, it will make the point come through so much better…only to look up three hours later and realize it has led me down a rabbit hole.

Nothing will crush your ability to craft communications that generate emotion and desire more than going down that rabbit hole without some guardrails to keep you on the path. It's the reason I forestall going into PowerPoint until the absolute last moment—when I'm confident that I already know what will go onto the page.

---

[29] https://www.theguardian.com/music/2005/feb/26/popandrock.music

Your PowerPoint Guardrails

At this point, you're working almost exclusively in your slideware. You've settled on your big idea; you've storyboarded and outlined your narrative and blocked the titles and a space for your visual into your software. You've even started to doodle the visuals that will make your presentation memorable. Great! Now it's time to load your content.

I'm going to remind you again of the interior design metaphor. When you move into a house, one of the first things you're going to do is move all the furniture into the appropriate room, right? Beds and dressers go into the bedrooms. Sofa and gigantic flat-screen TV go into the den. Etcetera. Now, imagine if you were moving into a new house and you started with your bedroom, but instead of just getting everything into the house first, you took your time fishing through all of your boxes to find the sheets and duvet so you could make your bed. Then you went looking for the accent pillows. Next, you found the boxes with your clothes so you could put them neatly into their dresser drawers. You get the idea—it would be a painfully slow process. You might never move in!

Sadly, this is what a lot of folks do when it comes to creating their decks. They move their content (the furniture) into a page (a room) and then go about trying to perfect that page before moving onto the next. That's PowerPoint's gaping time suck.

To prevent you from falling prey to the siren song of PowerPoint and straying into the time suck, **TELL yourself that you WILL NOT FORMAT OR TRY TO PERFECT YOUR SLIDES IN ANY WAY until you've moved in all the furniture**.

PowerPoint Guardrails

1. Place your headlines and subheadlines approximately into the places where you blocked them earlier.
2. Transfer all of your subordinate copy into the speaker notes section. Don't put it on the slide itself.
3. Go through each slide and work on crafting and refining the visual(s) that will tell your story, then place it in the layout of the pages.
4. Work on your copy. See what you've got in your notes section and refine it so that it complements your visual, and the combination of words and images tells the complete story of that page.
5. Finally, add footnotes for sources or references.

Get the Furniture and Boxes into the Right Rooms

I've already talked about the power of being succinct in chapter 6, but I'm going to give you another friendly reminder now that you're in your slideware and you've got all that wide-open space!

Space implies clarity. For you to be perceived as an authority, you need to speak declaratively. Start by placing your headlines and subheadlines. Keep them short and make an impact. If you've already tightened your copy, go ahead and add that to the page now too. However, if you have a lot of copy or notes that you haven't refined yet, just dump it into your speaker's notes section for now. I use that as a dumping ground for all the info I'll need to develop bite-size copy for the page later, making sure to **boil it down to its very essence**.

TIP

Use your slideware's speaker notes section as your workshop until you've refined your idea. Resist dumping unorganized thoughts onto your slide.

But how do you deal with the reams of data that need to support your message? If you need considerable documentation to substantiate your conclusions, move that stuff into the "garage"—a.k.a., the appendix. The main pages of your deck are for making declarations, not for getting your audience to repeat the path you took.

TIP

In PowerPoint there's a setting where you can set the software to auto-size your fonts to fit the size of the text box you have. Turn that off. As you put copy on the page, you need to see how much space it actually occupies.

Assemble the Furniture

Sometimes you have to assemble a piece of furniture in the room because it's so big. Think of your visuals as those big pieces of furniture.

Take time to really craft and refine your visuals now. Build your doodles into presentation-worthy graphics. Condense your spreadsheet data into simple tables or charts. As Tufte would say, *Visuals should make the complex clearer and the point immediate*.

In some cases, as I've discussed before, the visual will be typography (a.k.a., you'll turn words into visuals). If that's the case, build those now. **By the time you've got your headings, subheads, and visuals placed, chances are that 90 percent of the message is on your page**. It might not be as perfect looking as you want, but your room (the page) is now livable. You can sleep on your bed, sit on your couch, or have your dinner seated at your dining room table.

Refine the Copy

OK, so now it's time to finalize your copy. **Since you've already got your headlines and your visuals blocked in, now you need to add** *just enough* **support for your reader or audience to get the point without you having to voice it over too much**. This is especially important if you're assembling a standalone pre-read deck.

Take some time to think about the meaning you want your audience to walk away with and write the words to suit. Make your best effort at writing copy—full sentences—that might actually come out of your mouth. **Keep it short and direct. Summon your inner Hemingway**. He was notorious for writing terse, straightforward stories, with short sentences that resulted in a sense of gravitas.

I know that many of you out there will say, "I'm a terrible writer," or "I hate writing copy." I have two things to offer at this moment. The first is in the form of tough love. Get over it! You once told yourself you couldn't ride a bike, you couldn't swim, you couldn't read, or spell, or drive. And then you learned how. So suck it up, buttercup, and get past that "no" so you can get to work. The second is that if you can communicate (and I assume you can, or you wouldn't be reading this book right now), then you can write. You may just need to unlearn how you've been instructed to write in the past. **There's no need to be clever or use big words. It's really as simple as saying what you mean.**

Something strange happens when we sit down at a computer and start typing, and I really don't know where it comes from. Nobody expects you to have more eloquent prose coming from your fingertips than can come out of your mouth. So if you're really struggling, fire up a transcription app on your smartphone and start talking. Call up a friend who has zero knowledge of what you are working on, ask for permission to put them on speaker, and record the conversation. Encourage them to ask questions until they 100 percent understand the material. Later, go through your transcript and start mining for the gold, because it's definitely in there.

Not so long ago, I took part in a course on finding happiness that two wonderful friends of mine facilitated. One section was about understanding your subconscious thoughts. I had a huge insight when they advised us to pay attention to our "blah blah" because often the "blah blah" reveals what we *really* think. The "blah blah" are *the things we say between the things we want to say,* and that's where our particular "truth" comes out in its most unvarnished form. So when you go back and review your recording, search for the "blah blah" because there are likely very clear and concise nuggets and sound bites you can lift directly.

Emotion Sells. Logic Justifies.

One common question I get in workshops I do is, "How do I inject emotion into a *fill in the blank* deck?" They usually fill the blank with things like "business case," or "status update," or "budget meeting," or "IT proposal," or some topic that seems like it would be dryer than burnt toast. **But emotion is everywhere; you just need to know how to spark it up and then make sure it has enough oxygen to develop**.

Here's the good news: you don't need to manufacture emotion for a presentation, because your POV (point of view) and the story structure itself will be the spark, and white space is your oxygen. Keep that page clean! Nothing will snuff the flame of a good presentation more than walls of words and complex data sets.

A presentation is sort of like a reverse mullet. If you were unfortunate enough to live through the period of time in the eighties when mullets were all the rage, you know it was a haircut that was "business in the front, party in the back." Well, a presentation is the reverse of that. It's *emotion* in the front and *logic* in the back. In a presentation, the front section needs to bring the emotional party to get the brain working toward justifying its emotions. The appendix is the container for all the complex logic.

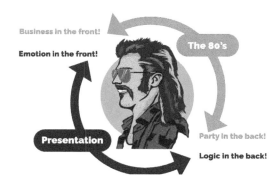

Business in the front!

Emotion in the front!

The 80's

Presentation

Party in the back!

Logic in the back!

Summing Up

There are some presentations that just speak for themselves. The story carries the reader effortlessly from page to page, and at the end the answer is obvious. The only way this happens is through careful planning and execution, and that's what you've just done. You should be able to read through your presentation and feel its ease. You may even get that terrifying feeling that you've oversimplified. You may ask yourself, "Is that really all there is to it?" Well, before you panic and start looking for ways to *complify* (my made-up word) your deck again, take a beat. What you've done is tame the beast, and that, my friends, *was* your job. It takes a lot of brain power and genius to do what you just did. **Austerity is beautiful because it refines things down to their essence, and what you've just done is peel the onion down to its beautiful sweet core**. From here on out, things are going to get really easy.

Just like in book publishing, when the manuscript is done, you send it to your editor and they get to work on designing and polishing your book into a form that's ready for the shelves. That's what you'll do next.

Key Takeaways & Homework

I get asked by clients all the time how to write better copy, and I have just a few maxims.

Presentation Copywriting Rules

1. Use full sentences.
2. Less is more.
3. Be human.
4. Write in plain English, no higher than about 10th grade reading level.

As you transition into working exclusively in your slideware, follow these guidelines:

▶ Save the editing for after you've moved in all the content.

▶ Place your headlines and subheads first, keeping them succinct.

▶ Move all of the explanatory copy to the speaker notes section.

▶ Refine and complete your visuals.

▶ Next, write the copy to support your headline and visuals.

▶ Take anything that's complex and stick it in the appendix.

▶ And finally, add in any sources or references as you go. Be sure to link to them from within the main document to make your document more usable (i.e., easier on the readers when they need to reference the supporting data).

Chapter 11
Designing Your Slides for Usability

How to build your slides for maximum
scannability to **enhance interest, attention,
understanding, and retention**.

The 15-Second Test

During corporate workshops I often play a game where participants try to comprehend the basic content of a company deck they haven't seen before. While the acronyms will be familiar, participants don't really know the meat of that particular presentation. Nancy Duarte would call this the STAR moment (something they'll always remember). I flip through the pages, with fifteen seconds per slide, and can see people's eyes glaze over around slide fifteen. They get anxious around slide twenty, and I often see them give up even trying beyond that. It feels like forever to them, and to me!

Once I get to the end of the presentation, I ask them to tell me what they learned. Here's what they say: *The presentation is about [insert topic]. They are asking for approval to move forward. They will need funding.* These are all generalities.

Then I bring the magic. I show them a version of the slide deck that we've reworked using all the principles you're learning in this book. There's always a palpable AHA! moment. I ask them what they learned. Suddenly emotions spring forth.

- ▶ *This project could have a tremendous impact not only on our bottom line but on the people we serve.*

- ▶ *Though it will take $XX million in investment, the return could be twenty times that.*

- ▶ *If we don't do something about this now, one of our competitors will.*

- ▶ One time, one participant said, *"If I had the power, I would write you a check right now!"* That check would have been for $213 million.

What Is a Presentation?

When you think about a presentation, what is it exactly? **It's text, images, colors, background. But when these elements come together in the right way, they move mountains**. Reading a well-crafted presentation feels effortless, and that's because it was designed to feel that way. Great presentations ignite an urgency to "do something about it." That's what stripping your message down to its essence does. But it also takes careful presentation *design*. **And by design, I mean intentional decisions that will make the presentation more usable**.

Look up any article on design and you'll see a few motifs repeated over and over again. Design is people-based; it's purposeful; it has integrity with itself and its use. **There's an element of restraint.** For presentations specifically, it's also helpful to look at print design, book design, and graphic design, where you'll come across additional concepts like balance, proximity, contrast, repetition, hierarchy, negative space, and such.

I stated earlier that when you're crafting your deck, you need to embrace your role as an author. You also started to wear the cloak of *designer* as you doodle your way to better and cleaner graphics. Well, now it's time to expand your role a bit more to embrace the totality of visual design, where you'll consider your typography, colors, balance, consistency, contrast, and so on.

Design Decisions: How Will Your Presentation Work?

Ultimately, your deck is a functional tool that you are creating to accomplish something, be it to inform or persuade. In many cases it will also be a physical artifact or tool. It might be a stack of papers quickly printed in black and white or a heavyweight spiral-bound collection of pages. So as you think about the packaging phase of your presentation, you need to make design decisions that further the functionality of the tool you are creating.

All design decisions should begin with empathy. What does your Hero need? How will they actually interact with your presentation? Before we get into specific decisions about typography and color, consider the following questions:

How will people engage with your presentation?

► Will it be printed? If yes, in color or black and white?

► Will it be projected in a room? What size room? Lights on or off?

► Will it be read on a computer screen or another digital device, like a tablet?

Knowing the answers to these basic questions will help you make a few key decisions early on. I'll point out places here and there where you might choose to make different choices depending on your answers here.

Typography

When considering typography, you need to **think about the design principle of readability, as well as consistency**. Keep it simple. Assuming you're creating a deck for professional use, don't veer toward quirky or "creative" fonts. **Funky fonts make you look like an amateur**. There, I said it. When you invoke fonts like comic sans and **IMPACT** and permanent marker and stuff like that, you look silly, and that's not what you want. Those fonts will actually distract your reader, and for the work you're doing, that's a cardinal sin.

The other reason to keep it basic is that **not all fonts play well with all programs**.

For example, even though PowerPoint is by far the most widely used slideware on the planet, I don't use it at all. If someone sends me a PowerPoint, I'll either upload it to Google Slides and view it that way or open it up with Keynote on my Mac. When you use specialized fonts, they often get converted to different fonts, and that can have some very strange effects. They sometimes occupy a different amount of space on different programs, even though the point size is the same. That results in your titles running off the page or drifting down into your body copy and other things that are a general pain in the rear for your reader.

TIP

As a rule of thumb, limit your fonts to two for your entire presentation. In some (special!) cases it might make sense to use three, but those are few and far between.

Serif or Sans Serif?

There are entire books on typography, but this is a deck you're building, not the website for the *New York Times*. That said, you should know what a serif is and when to use it. **Serif fonts are the ones with the little tails (serifs) on them.**

Serif fonts that are widely available on just about any slideware are:

Time New Roman
Garamond
Georgia
Cambria

See those little marks on the ends of the letters? Those are the serifs. They are considered traditional (older) but also have practical use. When you read things in tiny font, those little tails actually help your reader distinguish one letter from another. That's why you see them in newspapers so much. But we already covered that you're not re-creating a newspaper, and you're going to have plenty of white space on your pages, so in reality there's no need for you to concern yourself with serif fonts on the basis of readability. However (as you'll see later), you may want to use them for contrast.

Sans serif fonts (which literally means without serifs) are the widely accepted fonts for presentations. If you fire up your slideware and just start typing (which you did in the last few chapters), chances are pretty good you typed everything in a sans serif font.

On PowerPoint you'll see Calibri. In Keynote you'll get Gill Sans. And Google Slides will probably default to Arial. There are a few others noted below that work well with pretty much all slideware. You'll have to do a little digging if you're curious about others.

Calibri
Gill Sans
Arial
Helvetica
Verdana
Tahoma

But which ones should you use in *your* presentation? Well, first off I would strongly steer you to widely available fonts that can be rendered on just about any slideware. Don't spend too much time looking for the perfect font. **Your goal is simply to find a good readable and professional font that doesn't do weird things when your deck is opened up into different slideware. Common fonts are your friend, and you'll want them to at least be PowerPoint compatible**.

TIP

One way to 'embed' fonts into your presentation that will probably work in any presentation (and that won't cost you a penny) is to use Google fonts. Head over to fonts.google.com and you can see how each font renders the same text.

Combining Fonts

I mentioned earlier that two fonts in a presentation should be sufficient, but why would you even need two? Well, you may need two for contrast. For example, your headings and subheadings could be different fonts and different font sizes so the reader knows which to prioritize. Here's an example.

This page uses a combination of Arial (sans serif) for both the heading (H1) and the body font. But the subheading (H2) uses Cambria (a serif font in italics). The effect creates contrast, but since the same style applies to each slide, we also achieve repetition.

PERSUASIVE PRESENTATION SKILLS ARE SKILLS WORTH INVESTING IN.

Senior executives are short on time, need to consume vast amounts of information from direct reports, and are relied on to make huge decisions that can make or break the attainment of business critical goals.

In most businesses, decisions are made on the basis of the information shared in a PowerPoint presentation. And yet, very few who create presentations have been trained to develop a slide deck that not only facilitates a **coherent, and thoughtful conversation** — but that also makes it easy for the reader or audience to understand with ease, and to make **quick, confident decisions based on accurate and articulate information.**

At Zumaeta Group, we train teams to develop **clear, concise presentations that transform audiences for accelerated decision-making** in marketing and sales environments.

We believe in the power of presentations to facilitate **game-changing conversations**, to produce **off-the-page insights**, and to produce the kind of **clarity that compels decisive action.**

Here's how we do it.

- In a workshop setting, we first **train your team on the fundamentals** of persuasive presentations, and how to use frameworks to find the right narrative.
- Then we **guide your teams through workshopping a presentation** they are actively working on.
- At the conclusion of the workshop, **participants present their slide decks** and get LIVE feedback.
- After the workshop we **work with your teams on an ongoing basis on mission-critical presentations** to refine their skills, enhance their delivery, move projects forward.
- We also assist leaders with **comprehensive presentation development** for game-changing projects and initiatives.

11

This page uses lowercase text for the H1. Lately, I'm tending toward all lowercase text because it is much easier for the eyes to scan.

Persuasive presentation skills are skills worth investing in.

Senior executives are short on time, need to consume vast amounts of information from direct reports, and are relied on to make huge decisions that can make or break the attainment of business critical goals.

In most businesses, decisions are made on the basis of the information shared in a PowerPoint presentation. And yet, very few who create presentations have been trained to develop a slide deck that not only facilitates a **coherent, and thoughtful conversation** — but that also makes it easy for the reader or audience to understand with ease, and to make **quick, confident decisions based on accurate and articulate information.**

At Zumaeta Group, we train teams to develop **clear, concise presentations that transform audiences for accelerated decision-making** in marketing and sales environments.

We believe in the power of presentations to facilitate **game-changing conversations,** to produce **off-the-page insights,** and to produce the kind of **clarity that compels decisive action.**

Here's how we do it.

- In a workshop setting, we first **train your team on the fundamentals** of persuasive presentations, and how to use frameworks to find the right narrative.
- Then we **guide your teams through workshopping a presentation** they are actively working on.
- At the conclusion of the workshop, **participants present their slide decks and** get LIVE feedback.
- After the workshop we **work with your teams on an ongoing basis on mission-critical presentations** to refine their skills, enhance their delivery, move projects forward.
- We also assist leaders with **comprehensive presentation development** for game-changing projects and initiatives.

And this is the same page again, with all the same fonts, except the H2 has been bolded instead of italicized.

Any of these three styles work. It's a matter of personal preference. But you can see that all these "looks" were achieved with just two fonts, a sans serif and a serif.

Persuasive presentation skills are skills worth investing in.

Senior executives are short on time, need to consume vast amounts of information from direct reports, and are relied on to make huge decisions that can make or break the attainment of business critical goals.

In most businesses, decisions are made on the basis of the information shared in a PowerPoint presentation. And yet, very few who create presentations have been trained to develop a slide deck that not only facilitates a **coherent, and thoughtful conversation** — but that also makes it easy for the reader or audience to understand with ease, and to make **quick, confident decisions based on accurate and articulate information**.

At Zumaeta Group, we train teams to develop **clear, concise presentations that transform audiences for accelerated decision-making** in marketing and sales environments.

We believe in the power of presentations to facilitate **game-changing conversations**, to produce **off-the-page insights**, and to produce the kind of **clarity that compels decisive action**.

Here's how we do it.

- In a workshop setting, we first **train your team on the fundamentals** of persuasive presentations, and how to use frameworks to find the right narrative.
- Then we **guide your teams through workshopping a presentation** they are actively working on.
- At the conclusion of the workshop, **participants present their slide decks** and get LIVE feedback.
- After the workshop we **work with your teams on an ongoing basis on mission-critical presentations** to refine their skills, enhance their delivery, move projects forward.
- We also assist leaders with **comprehensive presentation development** for game-changing projects and initiatives.

10

Font Sizes

There is so much out there about what the right font size is. I once heard an outstanding presentation from Guy Kawasaki in my early days in corporate America—he espoused his 10/20/30 rule of PowerPoint. The idea was that you should have ten slides that take you no more than twenty minutes to present, and you should use a minimum of thirty-point font. I love Guy and have many of his books on my bookshelf, but that was back in 2005![30] I'd like to believe that if you had a longer discussion with him, he might say more.

The thing is, PowerPoint isn't used solely for what we traditionally thought of as presentations anymore. If I was a betting person, I'd say PowerPoint (and other slideware) has overtaken Word and other classic word processing software. So we need to think of font size beyond a "presenting" context. I don't believe in hard-and-fast rules, but I do believe in guidelines. **10/20/30 is a great guideline if you're presenting to a large room. In other contexts, it's less practical**.

---

[30] At least that's the oldest reference I can find on his website, https://guykawasaki.com/the_102030_rule/

In my experience, **starting with the "body" text size makes the most sense**, as it will be the smallest text on your page that potentially contains the bulk of the word density. A good rule of thumb is to first consider how far your audience will be from the screen to determine a comfortable text size. For example, let's say your audience will read your slides as a pre-read (prior to the actual presentation) on a laptop or tablet whose screen is about thirteen inches wide. Well, in this instance the reader is likely reading at about eighteen to twenty-four inches away from the screen. **These days, a rule of thumb for creating responsive websites[31] is that your body font size should be at least 16 pixels (px)**. I think this rule translates very well to slides that people will read on a personal device, because the reality is that everyone's settings are different. Rarely do folks have their device set to view decks at 100 percent. Instead, they use the "fit" setting, but fit is relative to the screen size, so it's a bit of a crapshoot. 16px is obviously bigger than the standard email or document size, but decks should be less text dense than a document. So, if your body copy is 16px, your H2 might be 22px, and your H1 could be 30px.

[31] Responsive websites are those that are built to be able to shrink down to your phone size and not break.

You get the idea. You just want to make sure there is a clear hierarchy of information, and an obvious difference between the font sizes. If you have footnotes and little annotations, those could be 12px or even lower. **Start with your body copy size and then work up and down from there.** Here's an example using the pixel sizes I've talked about here that could work for documents read on a personal device.

This H1 headline is at 30px. It's the biggest text on the page and will be the first thing your reader reads.

This H2 subheadline is 22 px. It's clear that it's subordinate to the headline, but also superior to the body text to the right.

This is a paragraph at 16px. In most cases, this is about as small as you will ever want to get for body copy in a deck. It works nicely for decks that will be read on a personal device such as a desktop computer, laptop, tablet or even a smartphone.

Of course, if you were going to project this onto a very large screen, and people were going to be reading it from dozens of feet away, this would be too small.

Of course, if you're projecting your slides onto a screen in a conference room, or even a screen on a stage, everything changes. In that case, you'll want to make everything bigger. The rule of thumb here is to use your screen size and room size as your guide. One simple way to determine the right font size is to simply do your homework by scouting the room itself. Garr Reynolds says to *design for the back of the room*[32], so if you have the opportunity to do a trial run, simply project a slide onto the screen and go to the back of the room. Can you read the body text? If not, make it and everything else proportionally bigger until you can.

If you don't have an opportunity to scout in advance, then use Nancy Duarte's rule of thumb. Take whatever screen you're building your slides on and measure the screen on the diagonal. (For example, my MacBook Pro laptop screen is 13.3 inches on the diagonal). Then launch your presentation into full-screen mode and go stand 13.3 feet away from the screen. Can you read it? If not, make everything bigger until you can.

---

[32] Reynolds, Garr. Presentation Zen : Simple Ideas on Presentation Design and Delivery. Berkeley, CA :New Riders, 2012.

Color

OK, let's talk about color. As with all things we've discussed, less is more. If you work for a corporation, your colors are likely already defined. In fact, you might even have a complete style guide. In that case you won't need to decide which colors to use, though you may still need to decide how many of the style guide colors you want to put to work.

First, I'm going to assume that most of the presentations you're making are workaday presentations, in which case you'll have dark fonts against a mostly light or white background. So **when you consider the font colors, my recommendation is to use two, and in some cases three**. (I'm not counting instances where you'll have white on dark backgrounds). Your core font will probably be black or something very close to it. Your next color will probably be a brand color—assuming it's a dark color and has high contrast with your light background. And finally, you may want to have an accent color that you use very selectively to draw attention to key concepts. These colors should also loom large in your visuals as well as charts, graphs, and tables.

When you're deciding colors, you also need to think about basic ADA guidelines. Choose a mix of reds and greens and you'll leave all of your color-blind colleagues behind. Eight percent of men are color blind (while only one in two hundred women are), so make sure that you're picking colors everyone can actually discern. In fact, for fully accessible slides, you'll want to steer clear of colors being

the single indicator for interactive elements like links to other slides, footnotes, etc. In those cases you'd do well to use bold, add an asterisk, or introduce a consistent icon to indicate an interaction.

Below are a few font colors that are fully ADA compliant.[33]

[33] Color | Accessibility Guidelines

Colors on a White Background

#112e51 on #ffffff   #205493 on #ffffff

#0071bc on #ffffff   #205493 on #ffffff

#046b99 on #ffffff   #2e8540 on #ffffff

#4c2c92 on #ffffff   #212121 on #ffffff

#323a45 on #ffffff   #5b616b on #ffffff

#494440 on #ffffff   #981b1e on #ffffff

#cd2026 on #ffffff   #e31c3d on #ffffff

The US Web Design System, an official site of the US Government, even has guidelines for getting the proper contrast in your color system.[34] If you're creating your presentations in color but expect that readers may print black-and-white copies of your documents, these guidelines will ensure that readers can see what you mean to tell them. For high-stakes and especially long presentations with lots of data I'd recommend you print a black and white copy of your deck and review it to ensure the information is clear. High contrast paired with good labeling is your friend.

But let's say the world is your oyster and you get to design your own color palette. I love to pick colors that will complement the main character in the deck. For example, if you have physical products, you can likely get your inspiration from the package design. Or if you're in the services business, there may be colors that are associated with the industry. Regardless of what you decide, there are color theory guidelines that you can employ to find a pallet of colors that will work together.

[34] https://designsystem.digital.gov/design-tokens/color/overview/

Take a look at the color wheels below. Notice that there are several ways of combining colors that work well together. Isaac Newton first conceived of the color wheel when studying the effects of light through a prism in the early seventeen hundreds. Goethe later refined the wheel in the early eighteen hundreds when he studied the physiological effects of color.

In other words, there's science behind color theory! There are many tools and websites available to pair colors together in a way that is pleasing.

Let's look at how this might play out with four examples.

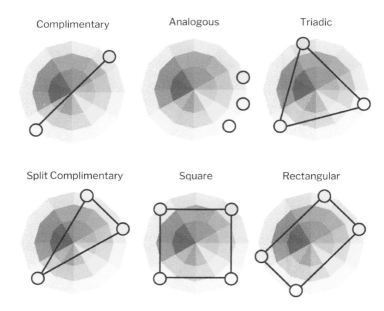

Complimentary   Analogous   Triadic

Split Complimentary   Square   Rectangular

Agriculture

Barley Corn	Green Kelp	Lola	Irish Coffee
#A19B62	#1B2E21	#DCD4DA	#5C3124

This is an agriculture example (Helvetica 30, dark gray)

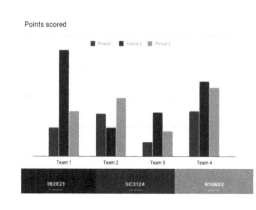

Points scored

*I'm going to make a subtitle the Irish Coffee color. That will be my **dominant color**, because it yields the highest contrast to my primary dark gray font. (Georgia 22)*

The way I've accomplished this color palette is by entering the photograph into a color palette generator. It's taken the colors in the photograph to produce a palette that is compatible. You can see intuitively that the colors suit the industry.

- I've switched back to Helvetica 16 for this paragraph to stay consistent with the principle of consistency.

- I've used one of the complementary colors (Barley Corn) to bring attention (contrast) to a discreet list of items. It's the color of the bullets

- I could use all of the colors to build graphs.

- I've opted not to use the lightest color at all since I'm using a white background, which comes in handy because it doesn't cause problems when I place charts that also have a white background.

10

Grilling

Lunar Green	Tumbleweed	Bud	Regent Gray
#454C44	#DDA17E	#9FB09D	#919CAC

This is a grilling example (Helvetica 30, dark gray)

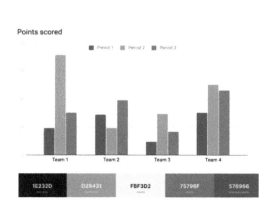

*I'm going to make a subtitle the Deep Space Sparkle color. That will be my **dominant color**, because it yields the highest contrast to my primary dark gray font. (Georgia 22)*

The way I've accomplished this color palette is by entering the photograph into a color palette generator. It's taken the colors in the photograph to produce a palette that is compatible. You can see intuitively that the colors suit the industry.

- I've switched back to Helvetica 16 for this paragraph to stay consistent with the principle of consistency.

- I've used one of the complementary colors (Harvest Corn) to bring attention (contrast) to a discreet list of items. It's the color of the bullets

- I could use all of the colors to build graphs.

- I've opted not to use the lightest color at all since I'm using a white background, which comes in handy because it doesn't cause problems when I place charts that also have a white background.

13

269

Health Care

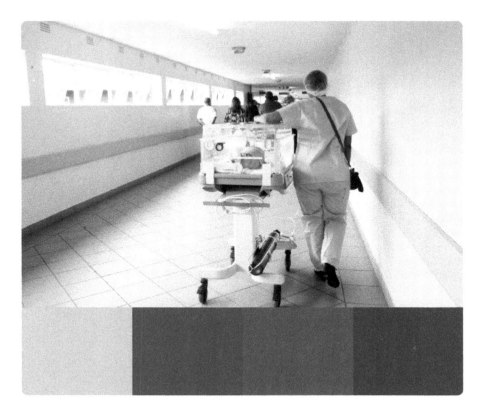

Pumice	San Juan	Crocodile	Pine Cone
#CBCFCC	#345B79	#77755B	#6C5D51

This is a health care example (Helvetica 30, dark gray)

Points scored

*I'm going to make a subtitle the Deep Space Sparkle color. That will be my **bdazzled blue**, because it yields the highest contrast to my primary dark gray font. (Georgia 22)*

The way I've accomplished this color palette is by entering the photograph into a color palette generator. It's taken the colors in the photograph to produce a palette that is compatible. You can see intuitively that the colors suit the industry.

■ I've switched back to Helvetica 16 for this paragraph to stay consistent with the principle of consistency.

■ I've used one of the complementary colors (gold fusion) to bring attention (contrast) to a discreet list of items. It's the color of the bullets

■ I could use all of the colors to build graphs.

■ I've opted not to use the lightest color at all since I'm using a white background, which comes in handy because it doesn't cause problems when I place charts that also have a white background.

14

Of course, you could also go for something bold simply by starting with a primary color and finding complementary colors.

Bold

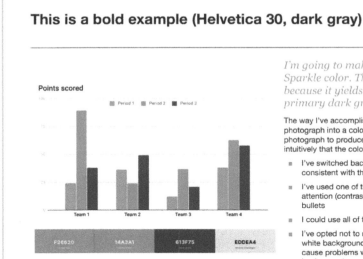

This is a bold example (Helvetica 30, dark gray)

*I'm going to make a subtitle the Deep Space Sparkle color. That will be my **viridian green**, because it yields the highest contrast to my primary dark gray font. (Georgia 22)*

The way I've accomplished this color palette is by entering the photograph into a color palette generator. It's taken the colors in the photograph to produce a palette that is compatible. You can see intuitively that the colors suit the industry.

- I've switched back to Helvetica 16 for this paragraph to stay consistent with the principle of consistency.
- I've used one of the complementary colors (orange red) to bring attention (contrast) to a discreet list of items. It's the color of the bullets
- I could use all of the colors to build graphs.
- I've opted not to use the lightest color at all since I'm using a white background, which comes in handy because it doesn't cause problems when I place charts that also have a white background.

15

Background

As you can see, **I favor white as a background**. This is mostly for logistical reasons. When I bring in new graphics and illustrations, it removes the hassle of trying to match background colors.

The primary decision you need to make is light versus dark, and the biggest deciding factor is whether you will present from a projector or other large screen into a largish room, or whether readers will read on a personal screen. If they're going to get the deck in their inbox and then read it on a personal device, the light background is the way to go. This is the way most presentations will be consumed. Here, your use of dark backgrounds will be very minimal—primarily for transitions and pattern interrupts.

On the other hand, if you're speaking from a stage or some other large venue, a dark background may be the right choice (though not in all cases). If you're going to be in a large room giving a presentation where you will be the star of the show and the slides will complement your live presentation, a dark background could be the right choice, especially for dramatic effect. Here are a few examples where that would work. As you can see, the slides reinforce the concepts, but they don't convey the entire narrative.

Covid changed everything.

People are demanding information, fast.

Economists and futurists predict by the year 2050, **infectious diseases will be the number one killer in the world**, surpassing heart disease. The enemies are stealthy – viruses, bacteria, fungi, parasites. They're caught. They spread. They evolve. Science must keep up.

Texas Biomedical Research Institute, 2015

Visuals

Diagrams, Charts, and Graphs

You've already learned that for charts and graphs, it's best to use the colors in your palette. The same goes for diagrams and illustrations. However, for simplicity's sake, I love to reduce things even more. There's a simple elegance to creating diagrams with only two colors. It forces you to put the attention exactly on what you want your reader to see.

One of the most impactful representations of data I've ever seen is the visual representation of Napoleon's Russian campaign in 1812–1813 drawn by Charles Menard in 1869! It's considered by many to be the greatest statistical representation of data of all time. The flow map depicts the folly of Napoleon's campaign in a way that is immediate. Napoleon had amassed over four hundred thousand soldiers as he entered Russia, and you can see the brown line get thinner and thinner the farther they marched. At the point they reached Moscow (which the Russians had abandoned temporarily) there were only a hundred thousand French troops, and the temperature was falling. The black line depicts the retreat, and by the time the French army crossed the Russian border back into Poland, there were only about ten thousand troops remaining.

If you look even closer, you'll see additional levels of information. Beyond the size of the troops and the distance traveled, there is also the temperature the army faced at various dates on its retreat. It's remarkable to grasp not only Napoleon's troops' dramatic decline as they marched farther and farther into Russia and back, but also the ability of a statistical representation to evoke an emotional response. There is an entire story in this two-color graphic.

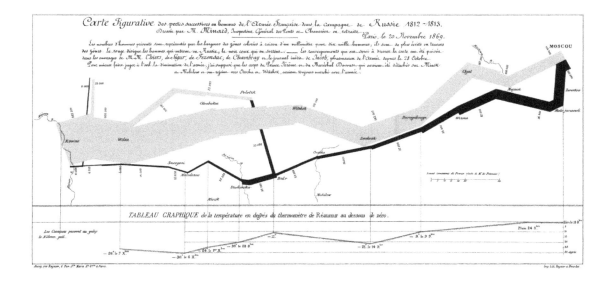

When you're creating visuals, simplicity and streamlining are the name of the game. Your objective is to get the meaning across as quickly as possible. I adore Edward R. Tufte's fascination with *Envisioning Information.* He's been called the Leonardo Da Vinci of data, and in his book Envisioning Information, he aptly observes that most of the time, surplus visual elements are "non-information, noise and clutter."[35] The key to graphics is to tell a story.

The same principles can apply to your basic charts and graphs as well. Emarketer makes distinctive infographics by almost always using only two colors.

Leading Virtual Selling Mistakes According to Buyers Worldwide, June 2020
% of respondents

Experiencing technology problems
89%

Using poor or no visuals during online meetings
86%

Not responsive to my questions or concerns
84%

Not prepared
83%

Lacking presentation skills
80%

Sending poorly written emails
80%

Distracted (by notifications, people, external disturbances, etc.)
77%

Making an unprofessional impression
75%

Note: experienced at least sometimes
Source: RAIN Group, "Virtual Selling Skills & Challenges," June 25, 2020
256796   www.e**Marketer**.com

[35] *Envisioning Information,* 1990, Edward R. Tufte

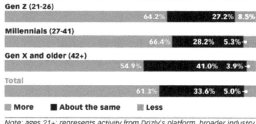

Alcohol Purchase Behaviors Among US Adults Since the Coronavirus Pandemic*, by Generation, June 2020
% of respondents in each group

Gen Z (21-26)
64.2% | 27.2% | 8.5%

Millennials (27-41)
66.4% | 28.2% | 5.3%

Gen X and older (42+)
54.9% | 41.0% | 3.9%

Total
61.3% | 33.6% | 5.0%

■ More ■ About the same ■ Less

Note: ages 21+; represents activity from Drizly's platform, broader industry metrics may vary; numbers may not add up to 100% due to rounding;
*March 2020
Source: Drizly, "Consumer Survey Report 2020," June 25, 2020
256806   www.eMarketer.com

Let's borrow an example from eMarketer to explicitly tell the story of how problematic using poor visuals during online meetings is. In this case, we would reduce everything else visually, spatially, etc.

279

In the original example, the heavy font that labels each data point fights with the heavy black bar for attention. The mix of data labels inside and outside the graphic is inconsistent. And no specific item draws your attention. Now look at the redesign, which tells an instant story because it eliminates anything that doesn't contribute to the takeaway.

This "less is more" principle could also apply to diagrams. Often, a simple two-color diagram could bring the story into sharp focus in a way that a more detailed diagram wouldn't be able to. In fact, even one color could do in some cases.

Virtual Selling Mistakes
According to Buyers Worldwide (June 2020)
% of respondents

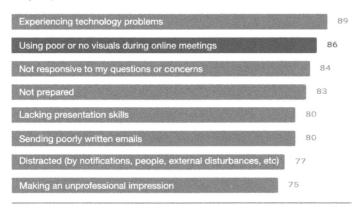

Experiencing technology problems	89
Using poor or no visuals during online meetings	86
Not responsive to my questions or concerns	84
Not prepared	83
Lacking presentation skills	80
Sending poorly written emails	80
Distracted (by notifications, people, external disturbances, etc)	77
Making an unprofessional impression	75

SOURCE: Data is from the June 2020 RAIN Group report titled "Virtual Selling Skills & Challenges." 528 buyers and sellers worldwide were surveyed online during Q2 2020.

Tables

Tables help categorize information in a way that allows your reader to see detail. But too often the tables you see in presentations are simply "cut and pastes" from spreadsheet software.

Here's the problem with tables. Often, you look to a table of data to find information that gives you an insight. This is what business intelligence really is. Then you drop that table into a slide without much further work. The problem is that you're asking your reader to work for the insight. That's a no-no in presentations.

This is a table cut and pasted directly from Google Sheets with data regarding COVID-19 cases reported from January 11, 2020, to July 28, 2020. I downloaded the raw data from the World Health Organization. It's not immediately intuitive or insightful.

WHO_region	SUM of Cumulative_cases	SUM of Cumulative_deaths
AFRO	21975007	441598
AMRO	392380358	18895992
EMRO	74460265	1933853
EURO	246062231	19386141
Other	118638	1794
SEARO	55206075	1459912
WPRO	26428920	934421
Grand Total	816631494	43053711

The first thing I'm going to do is make those regions and the column titles a little more intuitive by indicating the region (first column) in plain English. I'll also add commas to the numbers to make them easier to read.

Region	Cumulative Cases	Cumulative Deaths
Africa	21,975,007	441,598
Americas	392,380,358	18,895,992
Eastern Mediterranean	74,460,265	1,933,853
Europe	246,062,231	19,386,141
Southeast Asia	55,206,075	1,459,912
Western Pacific	26,428,920	934,421
Other	118,638	1,794
	816,631,494	43,053,711

But I still don't see a story here. What is there to understand from this table? One thing I might want to point out is that while the Americas had the largest number of cumulative cases at the point I downloaded this data, Europe had the highest number of deaths. And sure, while close study could have led the reader to that conclusion, it's a lot easier to see with a little help. I also added the data range directly into the table in case someone else were to cut and paste it later.

Region	Cumulative Cases*	Cumulative Deaths*
Africa	21,975,007	441,598
Americas	392,380,358	18,895,992
Eastern Mediterranean	74,460,265	1,933,853
Europe	246,062,231	19,386,141
Southeast Asia	55,206,075	1,459,912
Western Pacific	26,428,920	934,421
Other	118,638	1,794
	816,631,494	43,053,711

*COVID-19 cases reported from 1/11/2020 to 7/28/2020

Photography

Photography can be a blessing and a curse in presentations. On the one hand, there's nothing quite like a photograph to elicit an emotion, but when you pick a cheesy photo, that emotion might not be so great. You need to be intentional in how you use photography. If you don't already have an image library, you may want to begin to build one.

Look for sets of photographs that have similar qualities and tones. You may even want to apply a particular filter to your photographs that ties them together throughout your presentation. Notice how the photos below are handled. The models are always either in black or white; they are in nature; and the photos have a soft light filter. And, while these photos were clearly all taken at the same time, they indicate how you could curate additional photos that have the same qualities.

One way to reduce the cheese factor of your photographs is to avoid conceptual photographs altogether and opt for photos with an editorial style.

It's important to imbue non-type-based "ink" on your page with meaning that helps your reader. You want visuals to convey what you mean and no more. So, as with all things, reduce, reduce, reduce.

785 million people live without access to safe water

TIP

Make sure you have permission to use the photographs you select. There are all sorts of options for free photography. Georgetown University Library has some great guidance . [36]

[36] https://www.library.georgetown.edu/copyright/images-publications

Layout

Layout is one of the easiest ways to create consistency in your presentation and yet is one of the least employed techniques. I don't know why the slideware folks haven't figured out that they could help you a lot more by autoloading a grid system onto your page versus giving you a bunch of templates. Personally, I'm not a fan of the templates of any slideware because they can result in a bunch of nonsense if you don't know why or how they were created in the first place.

Let's talk grids. We've touched on this before in previous chapters, but it's time now to really understand them. When creating a presentation, the first thing you have to figure out is whether you will do a traditional four by three layout (best if you know that it will be printed onto 11 x 8.5 paper). Otherwise most folks (and slideware) are going to default to wide mode, which is better for reading, whether it's on a personal screen or a gigantic screen at a conference.

Widescreen

This is wide-screen.

This is wide printed on 8.5 x 11 paper.

Persuasive presentation skills are skills worth investing in.

Senior executives are short on time, need to consume vast amounts of information from direct reports, and are relied on to make huge decisions that can make or break the attainment of business critical goals.

In most businesses, decisions are made on the basis of the information shared in a PowerPoint presentation. And yet, very few who create presentations have been trained to develop a slide deck that not only facilitates a **coherent, and thoughtful conversation** — but that also makes it easy for the reader or audience to understand with ease, and to make **quick, confident decisions based on accurate and articulate information.**

At Zumaeta Group, we train teams to develop **clear, concise presentations that transform audiences for accelerated decision-making** in marketing and sales environments.

We believe in the power of presentations to facilitate **game-changing conversations**, to produce **off-the-page insights**, and to produce the kind of **clarity that compels decisive action.**

Here's how we do it.

- In a workshop setting, we first **train your team on the fundamentals** of persuasive presentations, and how to use frameworks to find the right narrative.
- Then we **guide your teams through workshopping a presentation** they are actively working on.
- At the conclusion of the workshop, **participants present their slide decks** and get LIVE feedback.
- After the workshop we **work with your teams on an ongoing basis on mission-critical presentations** to refine their skills, enhance their delivery, move projects forward.
- We also assist leaders with **comprehensive presentation development** for game-changing projects and initiatives.

6

Notice that when a wide-screen presentation is printed onto 8.5 x 11 paper with the "fit to paper" setting, it will print with extra space at the top and bottom.

ive presentation skills are skills worth investing in.

:ives are short on
consume vast
information from
s, and are relied on to
ecisions that can
:k the attainment of
cal goals.

In most businesses, decisions are made on the basis of the information shared in a PowerPoint presentation. And yet, very few who create presentations have been trained to develop a slide deck that not only facilitates a **coherent, and thoughtful conversation** — but that also makes it easy for the reader or audience to understand with ease, and to make **quick, confident decisions based on accurate and articulate information.**

At Zumaeta Group, we train teams to develop **clear, concise presentations that transform audiences for accelerated decision-making** in marketing and sales environments.

We believe in the power of presentations to facilitate **game-changing conversations**, to produce **off-the-page insights**, and to produce the kind of **clarity that compels decisive action.**

Here's how we do it

- In a workshop
  team on the fu
  presentations,
  find the right n
- Then we **guide**
  workshopping
  actively workin
- At the conclusi
  participants p
  get LIVE feedb
- After the works
  teams on an o
  mission-critic
  their skills, enh
  projects forwar
- We also assist
  presentation c
  game-changing

If the print settings aren't adjusted to "fit to paper," the content will flow beyond the printable page.

Assuming you're working primarily in sixteen by nine for your workaday presentations (and that they will be read mostly digitally), you'll want to set up a grid system much like web designers set up grid systems. One very flexible grid for sixteen by nine is the twelve-column grid. Dividing the width of your page into twelve columns seems easy enough on the surface, but to use a grid properly, you're also going to need to create space in between all of those columns so your text blocks and images don't run up against each other. Rather than numb your mind with the math, I suggest you just download a grid from http://deckonomics.com/resources.

This grid is immensely helpful when laying things out. We've already marked off the margins on this one. Now decide how to use the interior. You could do that in all sorts of ways.

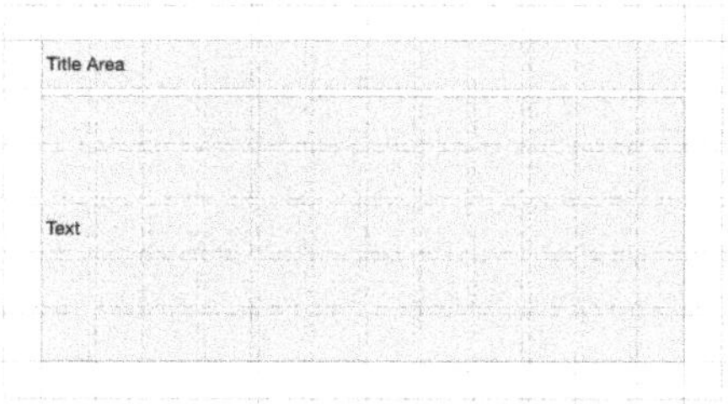

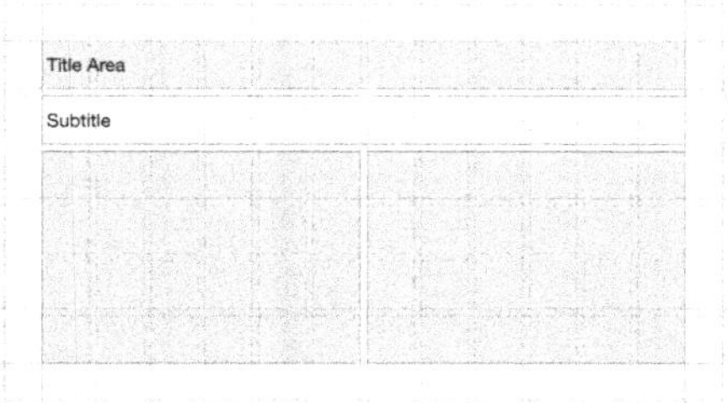

Title Area

Text

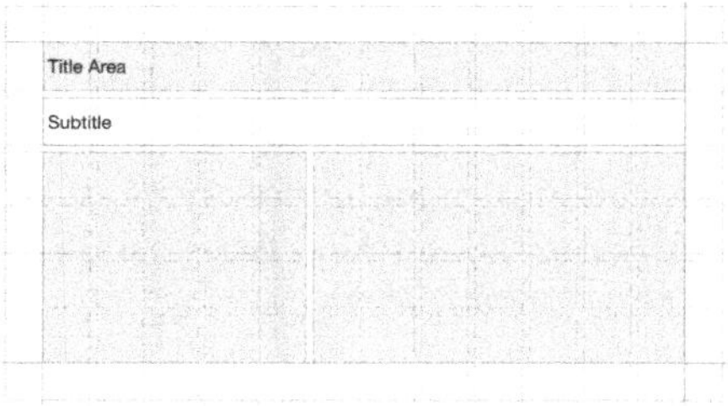

Title Area

Subtitle

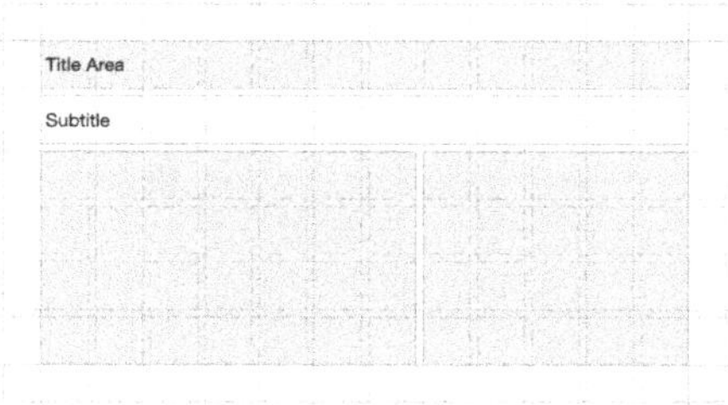

Title Area

Subtitle

Title Area

Subtitle

Title Area

Subtitle

Having a layout with continuity is one of the telltale signs of a professionally produced deck. If you follow the grid system, you'll get something that is more likely to be consistent. Nothing is more distracting than the location of titles and images moving around as you flow from page to page of your presentation. This is especially apparent when folks flip through your pages in a digital format.

Design Creates Usability and Confidence

The reason design is so important is that it makes your deck more usable. Your deck is really a container of information. Best-case scenario, your deck is consumed, then understood, and finally, assimilated. If you can accomplish these three things, you'll achieve some level of shaping your audience's understanding of a problem and the solution you're proposing. That's what you need to create confidence and will enable your audience to make a decision and to continue the story line.

But, if you don't get the design right, you'll create myriad speed bumps and off-ramps along the way that make your audience overwork to understand what you're trying to say. When your brain overworks, uncertainty creeps in. A well-designed slide has the immediacy required to keep the story moving.

Do You Need To Introduce Way-Finding?

For some especially long decks that have multiple chapters or sections, consider using way-finding in your deck. You've already seen earlier that I'm a big fan of using a table of contents at the start of the deck to lay out the story even if you only have a handful of slides. But if you have a deck where you'll be addressing a large body of work with clear categories, way-finding could be a way to ease the cognitive load for your readers and ensure that they always have a sense of where they are in the deck.

When I teach workshops, my teaching deck has hundreds of slides. There is so much content in the workshop that it helps if the participants understand where they are in their learning journey. To do that, I include a navigational element embedded into all the slides. There are five sections to the workshop, so each slide orients the participants to the section they are in. Use the colors of your palette to indicate different sections. You may also want to develop a transition-slide style to start each chapter. This will help prepare your audience for a new set of ideas.

TIP

A teaching deck is a whole other animal and while it uses the principles in this book, it also has to employ other types of slides not covered here to accommodate interactive portions of the day, table exercises, etc.

Develop Your Design and Style Guide

If you're creating an especially large deck, or you will create similar versions of deck, it's a good idea to create a style guide. All that means is creating a guide for yourself or others of the design decisions you've made. This differs from creating a template. While a template will give you various layout options and load-specific fonts, a style guide will give you a better sense of the decisions that you will have to make around colors, fonts, layout, photographic style, illustration style, and more.

Think about building a few slide masters that express the style for all of your decks. Here are a few things to consider.

▶ What grid system are you using?

▶ What color palette have you chosen?

▶ Where should the headlines, subheads, and body copy go for different layouts?

▶ Where will your diagrams and charts go, and what styles are they using (for example, label sizes, line weights, etc.)?

▶ What's the photographic style you've chosen?

▶ Do you have any specific navigational elements at work in your slide deck?

▶ Do you have a standard footer you need to include?

You get the idea. Build a guide that
indicates all these things very clearly.

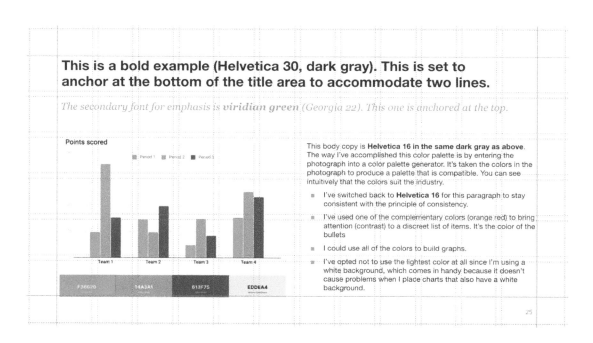

Get Eyes on Your Work

You absolutely must get other eyes on your work prior to finalizing and presenting or distributing the presentation. If you have the space, the best way to do this is to print all your pages and put them on a wall horizontally. This will enable your readers to see it as they would see it on a screen or printed page. Inevitably, your reviewers will catch little typos and spot inconsistencies in font, colors, or placement of various elements.

I like to **give reviewers guidelines**. I want to know if the headline made sense and the rest of the page supported the headline. I want to know where they had to puzzle over understanding something. I want to know what sent them down a rabbit hole of thought and whether the rabbit hole was helpful or a speed bump. What's most important, though, is to tell them you want to know everything, but may not act on everything.

Give your reviewers a set of highlighters and tell them to highlight the key point of the slide with yellow and use a darker highlighter to show where they got stuck, didn't understand something, or simply thought a part of the slide was superfluous. They could tell you they don't understand a slide entirely. If they do, make a note, thank them, and then decide whether you need to make a change. Don't waste time explaining. If they don't understand something, chances are pretty good that your intended audience won't either.

The Finishing Touches

Your deck has a job. Its job is to communicate your ideas in a way that makes them immediately meaningful, memorable, and actionable. But we humans are easily distracted. So take the last crucial step of reviewing your deck with a fine-tooth comb and get your colleagues to stress test its utility. This ensures all the time and effort you've spent designing and building your deck pays off in the end.

Let's revisit our house metaphor once again. You are the designer, and you've done either all or most of the building of the house that is your presentation. But your effort means nothing until someone "buys" the house. Now, before your prospective buyers decide to purchase, they're going to want to do an inspection, won't they? If you've ever shopped for a house, you know how easy it can be to become obsessed with little things. *Ugh, that wallpaper is awful. Linoleum—really? The closets are way too small. Oh my gosh, there's carpet in the bathroom!* It doesn't matter how good the bones of the house are; when home buyers find little things that tarnish the fantasy they had of the house before they crossed the threshold, those little things can make them question what sorts of problems the house has that they *can't* see.

So now's the time to make sure everything is just right so you can eliminate any cognitive friction that might come up as someone is going through your deck. Anytime I build a deck, a website, a sales page, an ad, or whatever, my goal is to make a slippery slide. I want my reader to glide from page to page without having to stop and think too hard. **Don't be that person who passes the intellectual work off to your reader. If your audience has to think too hard, it means you didn't think hard enough.**

A good book sticks with you and invites you to open it again and again. That's what you're going for with your presentation. **You want your deck to be the one that people WANT to print and keep on their desk as a reference**. When you can accomplish that, your stock will go way up in the minds of your readers. You will instantly become the domain expert.

Believe me, I've seen it again and again with executives that I've coached. **It only takes one great presentation for you to be the resident expert**. You just have to tell the story better than everyone else, and the process you've been learning will get you there every time. The trick is to make it look effortless. And in deck terms, that's scannability.

Usability Equals Scannability

► Scannability sets readers on a quest that makes them want to take a closer look.

► The final step is to package and promote the journey like a good travel agent would.

Now that you have a great "book" (deck), let's make sure it's built for spreadability and that you get the credit! In the next chapter, you're going to use the skills that great book promoters use to get their books to fly from the shelves and to get credit for their content.

Key Takeaways & Homework

▶ If you read nothing but the page headlines of your deck, would it communicate the complete story?

▶ Does each page communicate a single idea?

▶ Do your visuals tell the story of the headline?

▶ Review for concision. Find your wordiest page and count the words. Unless you're delivering a deck that will never get the benefit of your voiceover, shoot for less than two hundred and fifty words, and one hundred or fifty or less is even better.

▶ Is there enough white space on the page?

▶ If the readers were only to read the title, subtitle, and things that are bolded, would they get all the key concepts and insights?

▶ Is there continuity in where everything is placed from page to page? Fire up your deck in presentation mode and just advance quickly from page to page. If you see titles, footers, etc. jumping around, you have some fine tuning to do.

- ▶ Are your colors consistent and compatible?

- ▶ Are your font sizes consistent?

- ▶ Get someone to proofread your work! Eliminate any typos, as they distract and make you look sloppy.

- ▶ Look at your graphs, charts, and tables—does the data itself pop off the page, or is it the data container that has prominence?

Chapter 12

Enhancing Your Slide Deck's Spreadability by Thinking Like a Publisher

If you want your ideas to spread, you'll need to **package your deck to stand the test of time**.

The best decks are the ones that compel an audience to pass them— and the ideas they contain—to others. They're the ones that contain the ideas, insights, or puzzles that people talk about to their colleagues. There's a certain satisfaction in witnessing an idea that you've presented be spread by others. But hearing that someone else is trying to claim your ideas as their own? That's out of bounds. You may think that it's petty to think this way, but **authorship of ideas matters**. That's why books and other works have copyrights.

Another equally important reason that it's critical to attach your name to your work is so people who take up your cause can continue the conversation *with* you. They may have questions or new ideas. Or perhaps they've uncovered additional information that reinforces your work. Whatever the reason is, you've done them and yourself a disservice if you haven't attached key metadata to the deck that will help it live, or at least give it context in its moment in time.

Why Do So Many Decks Live Such Brief Lives? Let Me Count the Ways.

How many times have you toiled over a deck, spent dozens upon dozens of hours, presented it or distributed it, and then never looked at it again? Sadly, that's the life of most decks. They just don't stick. I know this from experience. It's especially true of the decks you email versus present. I can't count the times that I've put my heart and soul into a deck (that someone requested I prepare!!) and sent it off to the requester, never to hear a single word of response. I remember one multiyear project I worked on for a client where I felt like I was in some sort of Monty Python caper.

Let's call my client M. Here's how the years went. M would ask me to prepare a deck to describe the work I was doing.

M: *"Can you put together a deck that describes where we are now, where we want to go, and what we need to do to bridge the gap?"*

Me: "Yep, I can do that. It's a basic gap analysis and fits almost perfectly into the framework you've learned in this book so far. The Persuasion Journey™ is literally the blueprint for a gap analysis."

So off I went to assess the situation so I could build an evidence-based picture of the current reality. Then I did desk research and conducted interviews to conceptualize what the future could look like. And finally, I designed a killer deck and shipped it off to M. Then, silence for a few weeks until we convened a status meeting to report on how my team was doing to close the gap that we had pointed out in the deck.

M: *"This is great, Ginger. What would also be helpful is to understand where we're coming from and where we're headed."*

Me: Hmm, sounds a lot like my last deliverable. Did M read the deck? Should I shuffle the page order of that deck and resend it as if it was a new deck? Could I just put a different cover on the same deck and send it?

I could never tell whether M was reading the decks I sent. I would try to plant "Easter eggs" to see if M would catch them. Sometimes I would refer to specific page numbers of the deck where I had already answered the questions M was asking now. I would make bolder and bolder recommendations. It was like *Groundhog Day*. The entire ordeal was a bit "looney tunes" until I started proactively distributing my decks beyond M. Finally, the narrative gained velocity, and we started to get traction on the project. Why? Because we were circulating the information broadly, and M was getting the message from all sides.

So here's an admission. At that point in time, I had been working with this company for many years, and they had cajoled me little by little into doing decks their way. I had to force my narrative into an inflexible template, fill out preformatted pages, feed the deck through a specific pipeline, and anonymize it. I know now that doing all of those things was like giving my work the kiss of death. I also know that for some of you reading this right now, this is all sounding a little too familiar. But fear not; there are ways to get around frankly stupid rules. But first, let's examine why they exist in the first place.

The Curse of the Corporate PowerPoint

Corporations develop standardized PowerPoint templates to normalize how teams communicate. The intent is to both help the PowerPoint authors (so they don't have to reinvent how to present a progress report every time they build one) and also to help the audience or readers (so they don't have to relearn how to read the progress report every time). The intent is absolutely in the right place. But this practice also presents a few problems.

Templates are like a narcotic that numbs your senses while tricking you into believing that everything is great. Sometimes having a fixed template gives presentation authors a convenient place to hide. Take the progress report you see below. On the surface, this progress report is eminently helpful because you can quickly scan it for red flags and then dive in to see what the issue is. But what if your boss had instructed you to never, under any circumstances, put a red circle on the page? Sound crazy? It happens all the time. In the case below, a superior prohibited the deck's author from showing any red flags to the c-suite even though the second item was months overdue and should have been coded as "red." This is a prime example of hiding behind a template.

Product Launch: Roadmap

	Plans	Problems (Obstacles to Progress)	Progress	
Establish brand identity			• ROUND 2 video comments submitted to design team • ~~Brand guidelines drafted~~ • ~~Final logo selected~~ • ~~Script finalized~~	
Convert first 1000 registered users	• Determine drip campaign (if needed) • Plan acquisition campaign	• Will need to determine final pricing scheme • Need sign-up URL (register page) • Hi-res firm logos • Sample reports	• Landing page mocked up in CF • ~~Establish registration and tracking dashboard (Ohlen)~~	
Complete Series A deck	• Rough out pages needed			

Templates constrain an author's thinking. If you are in a situation where you are limited to a set type of slides, your thinking will simply not go beyond those constraints. If you're required to report on a project in terms of things that are on-track, off-track, and no longer relevant, that is exactly how you will see the project. What you won't see are the anomalies, the little surprises, and the competition that just lapped you, making your project dead in the water. Nor will you see opportunities you weren't looking for in the first place. If Spencer Silver had not told his colleagues at 3M about his failure to produce a super-strong adhesive that resulted in almost the exact opposite, a very low-tack adhesive, we wouldn't have Post-it Notes. Can you imagine? I'd be telling you to fill out index cards and to have a very long roll of tape.

Decks Fit into a Larger Context

The problem with templated decks is that the structure takes precedence over the ideas the deck contains. **The ideas you house in your deck will not spread if the deck is indistinguishable from every other deck in a company**. Without a proper book jacket, I doubt many books would be sold. For a presentation to matter, you need to know who authored it and when and why. What question did it seek to answer? What was true or assumed at the time the deck was authored? What role did the author play in skewing the narrative?

Suppose you read one of two decks on sleep habits. One is titled *Innovations in Sleep*. The other is titled *Why Sleep Matters Now More Than Ever*. Which one would you read? Now what if I told you that the author of one deck was a brain scientist and the other was a presentation put together by a billion-dollar bedding company? Which one would you read? Hard, isn't it?[37] Context matters.

One reason it's so important to include the deck's metadata is that without it, your work risks being exposed to a limited audience. If your colleagues aren't aware of your work, they can't benefit from it. Or they might undertake the *same* work all over again. Ultimately, more of the company's time and resources will be wasted. Building a deck isn't like chopping wood, with obvious and material evidence that the work has been done. Rather, designing decks is intellectual work, and in many cases leaves only digital traces. So to get your work out there, you're going to have to be intentional about it.

---

[37] These are both actually TED Talks, but one, *Innovations in Sleep,* is branded content created by Beautyrest, while *Why Sleep Matters Now More Than Ever* was created by Matt Walker, a brain scientist who studies sleep.

For Maximum Spreadability, Think Like a Book Publisher

The hint to gaining maximum spreadability for your deck is probably sitting right in front of you. It's right there in your favorite book. Pull any book from your bookshelf and take a look at the anatomy of a book and the information it carries. I pulled *Made To Stick*, by Chip and Dan Heath, from my shelf and here's what I observed.

The Book Jacket

The book jacket has key information like the title, subtitle, authors, and artwork that reinforces the ideas in the book. That's important! It also has a high-level executive summary on the back. Other books use authoritative blurbs (testimonials) that add credibility. It's more information that makes you want to open the book. They use the inside flap to introduce us to our mentors, Chip and Dan Heath. We learn why these mentors have authority. Stanford, Harvard, and Duke Universities—impressive.

Deckonomics

The Copyright Page

The "edition notice" or "copyright page" has all the hard-core metadata that one would need to understand this artifact in context. I won't go through the entire page, but let's observe a few things.

► The original copyright was 2007.

► The book was originally published in the US by Random House.

► The Library of Congress cataloging information gives us some clues to where this work sits in the context of all published works. Hmm, the primary category is social psychology.

Table Of Contents

The table of contents lays out exactly what each chapter will contain—a helpful preview of what I'll be reading and the flow of the contents. [38]

Table of contents

---

[38] Talk to any speed readers or voracious readers and you'll learn that they almost always read all of the jacket text, as well as the table of contents before deciding to read the book and also to get a quick summary of the book without ever reading it at all. I always take a look at the bibliography or index to see what other works are referred to. Almost all books stand on the shoulders of others' work. I want to know who those others are.

The Notes Section

This is like a bibliography and contains important information about what is validating the Heaths' points of view, claims, and so on.

The Index

The index provides a simple way to find ideas and topics that are sprinkled throughout the book. It's handy if you recall something of interest and want to refer to it later. I'll sometimes highlight lines in the index as a quick guide to pages I would have "folded" or to point me to where I've added marginalia.

Applying Book Principles to Your Deck

Now let's look at how we can apply some of the principles that book publishers use to enhance the spreadability of your deck. Most workaday decks will be read digitally, so make sure the digital file carries all the right information with it.

The Cover Page

Your deck cover should at the very least have four important things.

1) **A descriptive title** that tells the readers WHY they should open and read the deck. Notice I didn't say WHAT the deck is about. There's a difference between a deck titled "Consumer Strategy" and one titled "Captivating Attention-Deprived Consumers." "Consumer Strategy" doesn't really say much. It's better to make a bold statement, have a point of view, and get people's attention right off the bat.[39] It can also have a subtitle to further clarify the contents.

2) **A descriptive visual.** Many companies want all of their presentations to have a standard formatted cover page. That's just nonsense. And, while the graphically challenged might resort to using a cheesy clip art image, you won't be doing that. Find or create an image that will help your reader remember what your deck is about.

3) **The *author* or authors' names.** (If your company discourages putting the author names on the cover page, create an end page that has this information.) The reason to go with the author's name (rather than the presenter's name if they're different people) is for reference at a later date. If someone needs help understanding where the contents were sourced or the assumptions that went into creating the deck, the author has a better chance of fielding those inquiries than the presenter.

---

[39] If you're struggling with a good title, just head over to Amazon and type in your topic. Booksellers have to come up with impressive titles to move their books, so Amazon is a great place for inspiration.

4) **The date.** I prefer to use the date the presentation was edited (i.e., the last time its contents were actually touched) versus the date the presentation was presented (or the future date that it will be presented). I find it's more useful if I need to reference the document in the future.

There are two additional pieces of information that might be appropriate for the cover page or possibly the appendix. The first is the **"sponsor"** of the work (it could be your division or department in the company). The other thing that might be useful is the *version* of the deck that you're presenting. Often a deck you build will be a living document that, once published for the first time, evolves, or gets edited or augmented in some way. If that's the case, you'll want to indicate that so your readers can understand where they are in the artifact's lifetime. Borrow the "version of encoding" that software developers use. They'll label each major release of a software program: 1.0, 2.0, etc., with minor releases (bug fixes, minor updates, etc.) after the decimal. So, for example, if you realize your first major release has a few typos that escaped your attention on the first round, you could just name the next version that you release "1.1." Your readers will know that the version they're reading is substantively the same as 1.0 but with minor updates. Whereas if you added several pages or even chapters on a second release, you'd want to name that version "2.0."

Table of Contents

I'm a big fan of including a table of contents on slide decks for two reasons. One, **the table of contents substitutes as a great summary of the contents and if done the right way, can almost stand in for the contents themselves**. Two, the table of contents can also stress test how well you did at laying out your story sequentially and stress test the MECE-ness of your argument (mutually exclusive, collectively exhaustive).

Putting together your table of contents will be the very last thing you do, and it's easy. Simply create a list of all your slide page titles up to the appendix and indicate their page numbers. If you've got a really tight deck, you'll be able to read your list from top to bottom and get the entire gist of the contents. It will read like an elevator pitch (and sometimes, in fact, becomes the elevator pitch).

For the appendix contents, create a new column and simply list major sections of the appendix.

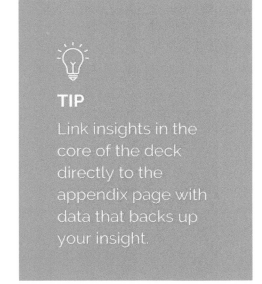

TIP

Link insights in the core of the deck directly to the appendix page with data that backs up your insight.

Executive Summary

Remember the information on the back cover and inside flap of the book where you got the equivalent of an executive summary of what the book contained? That's what your executive summary should be. It should be short and sweet but have the key elements of what you'll be presenting. You can do this in one of two ways.

Story Form

The situation: Obesity rates in America continue to increase.

The problem: Obesity rates are highest in non-Hispanic Black populations, who also have the highest prevalence of fast-food consumption.

The solution: Total Foods proposes to play an active role in curbing obesity in minority populations by offering affordable and healthy food options in small convenience marts focused on healthy quick-service food for the entire family.

Pyramid Form

Total Foods believes we can play an active role in curbing obesity in minority populations. Total Foods will launch a trial program of stores that:

▶ Are located in minority-dense neighborhoods

▶ Offer healthy food options with the same convenience as fast-food restaurants

▶ Offer healthy food options that are priced on par with fast-food restaurants

▶ Pack more nutrition into fewer calories dollar for dollar.

The idea here is to not overexplain. Just tee up what you'll be presenting in a way that gives your readers a reason to dive in.

Appendix

The appendix is sort of like the garage of the house. Or the attic. Or the basement. It's the place you put stuff you don't want to throw out because you might need it, but you don't necessarily need it right now. When I coach executives—especially the ones in science, health, finance, and other data-heavy fields—they constantly hear me say "put that in the appendix." Yes, the data is important. **But the data set is there for one purpose: to reveal an *insight that matters*. The insight goes into the core deck; the data set goes into the appendix**.

Your appendix should contain all the key data and information that users of your deck would need to have if they wanted to pick up the mantle of your work and carry it forward at another time, possibly without you. People move around, change departments, leave companies, and so on. But the product of your work should not die when you leave the company or the project. No one should have to retrace your steps exactly. So the appendix of your deck is where you'll put the metaphorical storage boxes of files for the next person to go through. This is where you'll put the equivalent of the copyright page, notes, bibliography, and index.

Deck Metadata

The first thing you should have in your appendix is the equivalent of the copyright page in books. On this page you'll want to list your authors and contributors and date the current version of the document was completed, and possibly the versions of this deck that came before it. Since your deck will be a digital artifact, I like to list and "link" to previous documents. You may also want to indicate who sponsored the deck. Who commissioned your work and would also have information about the topic?

References & Data Sets

All the reference material, data sets, and so on (all the boxes in the garage) will go after the metadata sheet. Depending on how complex your material is, there may be sections in your appendix. For example, you might have a section of financials that support your business case. You could have a section of case studies that support your claims. You might have a section of scientific data that supports your conclusions. And so on. If you have sections, just list the top-level sections in your table of contents.

The File Name

And finally, we have the file name. It's funny how often file names are personal.

▶ Q3marketingstrategy.ppt

▶ Mktgstrat-consumer.ppt

▶ PG12.19.20.ppt

▶ brandmtg-JV.ppt

These could all be the same exact deck, with different names that give scarce insight into the contents, the context, and so on. If you're like me, you've no doubt spent hours digging through files, looking for a specific version of a deck that had that one page that you need.

The solution to this is to design a consistent naming convention for files. Here are a few ways to do it, depending on your circumstances:

project_savedate_department_ authorinitials

This works well for a large company. For example:

▶ BCE_8.12.20_IMC_GZ.ppt

Or if it's an especially large project, you might even want to include the subtopic.

Project-subtopic_savedate_dept_ authorinitials.

For example:

▶ BCE-bizcase_8.12.20_IMC_GZ.ppt

Are you saving multiple versions in one day and feeling like you need to keep them all? No problem. Affix a version to the end of the date like this:

▶ BCE-bizcase_8.12.20.2_IMC_GZ.ppt

If you're like me, and you work with multiple companies, you can add the company to the beginning of the filename like this:

▶ KP_BCE-bizcase_8.12.20.2_IMC_GZ.ppt

You get the idea. The point is to **come up with a file naming convention that can help everyone make sense of the contents in your deck**, but also have a sense of the evolution of multiple files over time if they're looking through digital file folders down the line.

There's Power in a Deck That Sticks Around

I remember the first deck I did that changed everything for me. To be honest, it was rather late in my otherwise accomplished career. I had already won three Emmy Awards and over a dozen other awards as a television executive. I had built hundreds of decks along the way. But when I left the TV world to start my own consulting firm, I floundered for a while, trying to find my feet. I had a lot of knowledge, yes, but I didn't really know how to tell a story to a cold audience from scratch. Meaning, I didn't know how to use a deck to sell a project. It's the irony of consulting. You have to build the deck you don't get paid for in order to deliver the one you do get paid for.

Anyway, I finally sold a project to Kaiser Permanente, a large integrated health care company headquartered in California. It was 2012, and the US health care industry was frantically trying to figure out the implications of the Affordable Care Act (ACA), which would require all Americans to choose and pay for health care. I had a lot of experience in Hispanic marketing, so when I found myself in a casual conversation with a then-VP of marketing at Kaiser Permanente, she asked me to help with an assessment of the Hispanic opportunity. It was a big project, and I knew I needed to deliver a top-shelf deck to make an impact. So I studied great decks.

At the time, SlideShare still existed and had a number of outstanding decks posted publicly from the likes of Deloitte, McKinsey, and others. I created a veritable encyclopedia of the Hispanic population in all the markets where Kaiser Permanente had members. I detailed not only their numbers, but their language preferences, their psychographics, their experiences with health care in their home countries, and even the different ways various Hispanic subpopulations responded to advertising. Then I spent money printing extra-large full-color copies and binding them into an oversized spiral-bound book.

There was no way I could have predicted it at the time, but that spiral-bound book launched a consulting engagement that lasted almost ten years. And the amazing thing is that years after Kaiser Permanente had already taken a lion's share of the Hispanic market, I would still spot my spiral-bound book sitting on different executives' desks. It was sticky, all right, because it was made to be handed from one person to another.

Sign Your Work

Can we get philosophical for a moment? The Sumerian accountant that pressed marks into a clay tablet (currently the earliest example of a system of writing) couldn't have known as he pressed his forms into clay that his writing would be immortalized. But it was. But what's even more fascinating is that he signed his work![40] If you've gotten this far, you've worked hard to design a deck that will communicate something of importance to someone who can do something about it. What you've created will, whether you realize it or not, be contributing to history.

So take the time to package your work up in a way that will be useful. If you do, you'll find yourself being recognized as a domain expert. You'll be recognized as having had a hand in building what came next. You will extend your reach and increase your exposure. All it takes is a little bit of organization and a little extra time. But again, if you've made it this far, you've been doing this along the way.

Your presentation is your mark, your image, and even your legacy. Make sure it's the one you want to make.

---

[40] Harari, Yuval N. author. *Sapiens: A Brief History of Human*kind. New York: Harper, 2015.

Key Takeaways & Homework

- Think like a book publisher and take the time to properly package your deck.

- Include a cover page that communicates the reason to read the deck.

- Include an executive summary or table of contents that entices the reader to go deeper.

- Include key metadata like the authors, contributors, edition, publish date, etc.

- Use your appendix for data sets, references, bibliography, and other key data.

- Implement a file-naming convention that works for you and others.

Now you have the power (and the tools) to steer your ship, what will you do with it? We'll look at what you can do with your newfound powers in the next chapter.

Chapter 13

Keep It Simple

You can change the world with a humble business presentation.

When I taught marketing at UCLA, I would often begin the semester with a simple example of what marketing *really* is—it's about *perception*. I would hold up two of the silver rings I wore every day. One was a unique design that I purchased at a market in Taxco, Mexico, a colonial town born from one of the best silver mines in the world. I bought it for $5, and it came in a little plastic Ziplock bag. The other was a widely popular silver mesh ring from Tiffany. It came in their iconic "Tiffany blue" box and cost around $300. I don't know where Tiffany's silver comes from.

"What is the difference between these two rings?" I would ask. The answer, of course, is marketing. And in this case, the tangible expression of the marketing was the packaging. Which would you rather give or receive? A fine silver ring in a plastic bag that resembles the ones you see cocaine in on TV crime shows, or a fairly common Tiffany ring in its instantly recognizable blue box and white ribbon?

The moral of the story is that **packaging matters**. In fact, it matters so much that it drives the very value perception of the contents it contains. It's the Tiffany brand that signals quality, craftsmanship, luxury, credibility, etc., and no amount of logic and reason will overcome the difference between how it feels to get a ring in a Tiffany box versus getting one in a plastic baggie.

My point on the first day of class was that my students would spend the semester learning the finer points of integrated marketing, and at the end they would turn in a paper—an integrated marketing plan—that would show me how well they could apply their skills. Obviously, it would be in the form of a presentation. Would they submit their deck in the equivalent of a plastic baggie or a Tiffany box? The choice was theirs, but I guaranteed them that the plastic bag would NEVER get an "A" in my class, and likely wouldn't get a "B" either. Why? Because that's how life works. If the point of the class was to learn marketing, this lesson was fundamental.

We all want to do good work when we begin a project, don't we? So why don't we always submit work we're proud of? Because, as Newman from *Seinfeld* would say, "The mail never stops!"[41] The problem is the work never stops. We have to keep the production line moving. And because the work never stops, it's important to **change the way you do the work** to guarantee that you'll get a quality piece of communication every time. When you wipe away the muck of developing your deck, you'll realize that what you hold in your hands is the power to bring forth something extraordinary. You have the power to change and advance the arrow of history and the arrow of your own journey through life.

You've no doubt heard of the concept of the butterfly effect. It's the phenomenon where a tiny action in one place can produce giant downstream effects elsewhere. The theory is that a butterfly flapping its wings in one place could cause a typhoon someplace else. Well, the work that you do in a deck also has ripple effects. Sometimes you will deliver a deck that creates an outcome, and sometimes you will deliver a deck that doesn't. But either way, there are effects.

[41] See *Seinfeld* Season 4, Episode 18 for a quintessential Newman moment.

A PowerPoint Saves an $11b Navy Program

A friend of mine, a former navy test pilot, delivered the PowerPoint of his life when he inherited a program to acquire a fleet of new attack helicopters for the navy. Unbeknownst to him, a "flashlight" status report of his new project had already been delivered to one of the secretaries of the navy. It had red lights down the line. He didn't realize how much he was "on the bubble" until he got a terse fax with "SEE ME" scrawled over the report from the secretary. Kevin and his team canceled Christmas that year and determinedly pulled together a PowerPoint. What's remarkable is that the navy had trained him for this.

Few people know that test pilot school includes a class on developing and delivering PowerPoints for just the occasion that you find yourself delivering mission-critical information to a high-ranking officer. When they walked into the meeting, they couldn't have known that the secretary had already canceled his program for new helicopters. But by the end of the brief presentation, Kevin had persuaded the secretary that while progress was going poorly at the moment, his team still believed in the program's value and had a detailed plan to turn it around. The secretary delivered three magical words: "I believe you." Kevin and his team saved the $11-billion program; his admiral had saved face; and Kevin went on to become a communicator who would represent the navy at conferences worldwide. He did it by following many of the key principles captured in this book.

A PowerPoint Funds Lifesaving Drugs

Amgen is a global leader in biopharmaceuticals. One of their areas of research and development is cancer. It takes an extraordinary amount of effort (and money) to develop an effective cancer drug and bring it to market. So it's not surprising that the company leaders have to be very thoughtful about where they place their bets when deciding which of their developments will have the highest and widest impact in helping people. Guess how they take their request for funds to the funding committee? Yes, as a slide deck. When you're asking for several hundred million dollars to bring a lifesaving drug to market, you better believe they take care to package that presentation well.

And while you may not be saving lives, I invite you to think a little more broadly about what you ARE doing when you build a deck. And what you could be doing. Playing small is a disservice to your potential and to your contribution to society. So think about playing bigger. By now you already know how, but let's wrap it up in a bow.

Before You Open Your Slideware...

1. First, you have to wrestle the beast. Dump and clump. Get all of your ideas, data points, and insights onto sticky notes and start arranging them into natural groupings.

2. Stress test your understanding. Try your hand at sketching the six slide types to uncover new insights. Once you've pulled together all of your thoughts, move to storyboarding. Transfer your stickies into a sequence along the 12Ps of the Persuasion Journey™.

3. Once you've storyboarded your message, support it where needed by using the Pyramid principle. Doodle and sketch along the way for deeper insights.

4. Move to outlining your story. Craft your headlines and subheads. Dump all of your support points into the outline.

5. Get ruthless with your editing. Be succinct. Try to pare down your language now, before you transfer it into your slideware.

6. Check how you're doing so far by copy blocking your pages. Sketch out your slides on paper or on a paper-style app. Pay attention to layout. Think about how you can communicate beyond text.

7. Sketch your initial visuals.

8. Move your content into your slideware, starting with your titles and subtitles.

9. Build and iterate your graphics, making them as focused as possible. If it's a chart or graph, start by giving it a title and then make sure the graphic proves your claim.

10. Now write the rest of your copy. Remember to be as focused and direct as possible, without the jargon and shorthand. Remember to leave plenty of white space.

11. Once you've loaded all of your content, review your slides for usability. Is the information succinct and scannable? Is there a clear and consistent visual style that makes it easy to navigate from page to page, and section to section?

12. Now put the finishing touches on your deck. Think like a publisher. Make sure you have a compelling title, cover page, executive summary, and table of contents and have packaged all the metadata that needs to travel with the deck.

Presentations are the tangible representation of your thinking, so take the time to make the artifact of your thinking clear and engaging. The best way to author a deck that is meaningful is to use the power of both verbal and visual storytelling. Remember to think of how well children's books do this. Don't be afraid of being straightforward and using simple language. Embrace simplicity. Simplicity and brevity produce clarity. Who could have thought that the most famous equation in the complex field of physics would be so simple? But $E=mc^2$ is just that. It's simple and direct, even though it explains the mind-bending conclusion that mass and energy are actually the same thing. And in case you haven't looked at the original document, Einstein explained the entire thing in just three pages!

I hate to lean on old tropes, but remember to KISS your presentation. That's right. Keep It Simple Stupid...or as I prefer to say, Keep It Stupid Simple.

About the Author

Three-time Emmy Award–winning writer and producer <u>Ginger Zumaeta</u> advises companies on positioning and communicating big ideas. She's the founder and CEO of Zumaeta Group/ Motive3, a positioning and messaging strategy firm, and author of the forthcoming book *Deckonomics: Design Presentations that Spread Ideas, Drive Decisions, and Close Deals*.

Ginger has worked with some of the world's largest brands, such as Coca Cola, Verizon, Union Bank, Amgen, Anthem, Infinity Insurance, and many others. She's the winner of three Emmy Awards, twelve Muse awards, and a Gracie Award for her work in television, and has held positions as an adjunct professor at UCLA and Cal Lutheran in marketing and research. Her insights have been featured in publications such as Business Insider, TheNextWeb, Better Marketing, Storius, and Marketing Profs, among others. She's been a guest on The Business of Story podcast, and she's spoken about marketing and messaging on numerous stages, including Verizon's Hispanic Marketing series, the Latina Style National Conference, Union Bank's Personal Branding series, Kaiser Permanente's Annual Brand Conference, and the Promax National Conference.

Ginger leaped from an award-winning career at NBC to launching a strategic consulting firm that specializes in building challenger brands. Now, Ginger is leveraging her experience in storytelling and persuasion, along with her studies at the Wharton School on the neuroscience of business, to advise corporate teams in telling better business stories to move high-stakes work forward with clear and succinct presentations grounded in story structure and backed by brain science.

Acknowledgments

I owe a debt of gratitude to so many. Thank you to Howard Joyce, Ernie Arboles, Bruce Botto, Eric Battilega, Mhairi Strachen, Ara Balkian, Neil Littman, Zach Rosenberg, Kevin Switick, Paul Murasko, Fernando Ferrer, Mike Macceroni, Ranga Walaratne, Barry Kull, Kristopher Scott, Guillermo Mairena, Tauseef Salma, Spencer Miller, Stanley Anderson, David Reid, Ranajit Gangopadhyay, Josh Etkind, Dr. Chandana Unnithan, Orlando Joven, Aaron Reitkopf, Rod West, Sami Pippurri, Steve Ennen, Pawel Lopatka, Jerome Selva, Dave Bennett, Kimmo Dekel Shavit, Beth Lisogorsky, and Abhishek Kasturia for giving me your time and your stories as I conducted my research.

Thank you to my mom who is the hardest working person on the planet, and taught me the greatest career lesson of all, "If you want the job, first do the job." I wanted to be an "author," and so I wrote this book. Thank you to my father, who gave me my insatiable lust for learning and inspired me to go further than mere wondering. He taught me to seek answers, spot patterns, and to fearlessly be myself.

Thank you to Stacie, who is my person, my ride or die, my love, my life, my wife. You inspire me every day.

Printed in the USA
CPSIA information can be obtained
at www.ICGtesting.com
CBHW061654110824
12793CB00075BA/842